Uromastyx

John F. Taylor

Uromastyx

Project Team
Editor: Thomas Mazorlig
Indexer: Joann Woy
Cover Design: Mary Ann Kahn
Design: Patti Escabi

T.F.H. Publications
President/CEO: Glen S. Axelrod
Executive Vice President: Mark E. Johnson
Publisher: Christopher T. Reggio
Production Manager: Kathy Bontz

T.F.H. Publications, Inc.
One TFH Plaza
Third and Union Avenues
Neptune City, NJ 07753

Printed and bound in China,
08 09 10 11 12   1 3 5 7 9 8 6 4 2

ISBN 978-0-7938-2897-5

Library of Congress Cataloging-in-Publication Data
Taylor, John F.
  Uromastyx : a complete guide to uromastyx / John F. Taylor.
      p. cm.
  Includes bibliographical references and index.
  ISBN 978-0-7938-2897-5 (alk. paper)
 1. Uromastyx. 2. Lizards as pets. I. Title.
  SF459.L5T39 2008
  639.3'955—dc22
                          2008018631

The Leader In Responsible Animal Care For Over 50 Years!®
www.tfh.com

Table of Contents

Within the rocky outcroppings of the deserts of East Africa and the Middle East, there is a group of lizards that remain somewhat of a mystery to most reptile-keeping hobbyists. These incredible lizards—while not considered rare—are seen as few and far between in standard collections of reptile species. Whether their relative scarcity is caused by husbandry requirements or just the initial expense of obtaining them is not known. It is known, however, that they are amiable lizards that with the correct care can sometimes be said to provide pleasure to rival the sheer enjoyment of keeping a bearded dragon. They are the spiny-tailed agamas, also called by the scientific name for their genus, *Uromastyx* (or even uros by their fans).

Within the herpetoculture hobby/industry (the keeping and breeding of reptiles and amphibians as pets), there are hundreds of species that are kept with regularity. Generally the popularity of these species begins when a few are imported and people eventually figure out how to breed them. These "new" reptiles and amphibians eventually become available to the public at

Introduction

large. Given time, more and more people learn how to breed them success-fully, and there is an explosion of popularity. This eventually dies off until someone breeds a new color variety, and then the sales increase once again.

The *Uromastyx* species that haunt the eastern African deserts seemingly refuse to allow their secrets to become unlocked only to cause them to be listed among the fad lizards. While this remains true, the *Uromastyx* species are in most people's opinion brilliantly colored lizards that command much more than just cursory glance.

Acknowledgments

This book is dedicated to the old man who had me chasing skunks and running from the moon when I was a boy. Little did he know that I hung on every word when he was teaching me about the natural wonders of the world. This one's for you, Boats. I love you, Dad, and thanks for all the walks and talks we shared. Also to my family and Mrs. Lois McLarty, who believed in me just because.

Chapter 1

Natural History

I n this particular chapter we will be uncovering the mystery of the species generally referred to by the catch-all common names of uromastyx and uros: where they are found, what they eat in the wild, and how they are divided and described as species. All of this information is relevant to the keeper because uros are essentially wild animals. Knowing about your lizard's life in nature is critical to successfully keeping it as a pet.

Scientific Names

All known and described organisms from bacteria to redwoods have been given a two-word name by scientists. This system is called binomial nomenclature. These two words are the genus and species respectively. They are the words in italics you will see following many names in this book. The genus name will always precede the species name and will be capitalized. The species follows and is always in lower case characters. Occasionally the species name may give a clue as to where the animal originated from—e.g., the Egyptian uromastyx (*Uromastyx aegyptia*), or it may refer to its pattern—e.g., the ocellated uromastyx (*Uromastyx ocellata*). Some organisms have subspecies, which are denoted by a third name: *Uromastyx dispar maliensis*, the Mali uromastyx. By convention, after you use the genus name once you can abbreviate it to the first letter afterward; you can also abbreviate the species name to one letter when you are talking about a subspecies. For example, we can refer to the Mali uromastyx as *U. d. maliensis*.

Calling a reptile by its common name may lead to confusion when you are talking to someone who may be from a different part of the world or even from a different part of the country. There can also be confusion when talking about species having a similar appearance. For example, there are many green tree frogs, but only one is called *Hyla cinerea*. Therefore, when buying or inquiring about any species of reptile, you should know the Latin or scientific name of the animal you are talking about.

Taxonomy

Taxonomy is the scientific method of classifying organisms. The goal is to group together organisms that are closely related. There are different levels of relationships, starting with the broadest, the kingdom (e.g., all animals), and progressing to the most specific, the species (e.g., humans). In order, the major categories are kingdom, phylum, class, order, family, genus, and species, with many of these categories having subcategories. All reptiles are in the class Reptilia (recently called Sauropsida), and the lizards and snakes are placed in the order Squamata. Squamata has several subcategories (suborders), and one of these, Iguania, contains many familiar families of lizards, such as the iguanas, the chameleons, and the agamas.

The family Agamidae is a large family of lizards living in the Old World (except northern Europe and Madagascar). It contains over 350 species categorized in over 45 genera. Agamids—along with the closely related family Chamaeleonidae—are distinguished from other lizard families by the presence of teeth on the ridge of the jaw (acrodont teeth) instead of teeth fixed to the inside surface of the jaw (pleurodont teeth). The lizards in this family dwell in a wide range of habitats from deserts to rainforests, and they are absent only from very cold regions. Most agamids are visually oriented, having incredibly acute eyesight.

For this book we are concerned with only one genus, *Uromastyx*, of the family Aganidae. There currently are 15 species in the genus, with the first one described in 1775 by Peter Forskal as *Uromastyx aegyptia aegyptia*. Depending on where you reside, you may find the lizards in this genus sold under a few different names such as dabb lizards, spiny tails, spiny-tailed agamas, thorn tails, uromastyx, and simply uros.

Description

All *Uromastyx* species are extremely stout in appearance and have a sharp triangular head that is distinctly set off from the body. Physically speaking they are surprisingly similar to the chuckwalla (*Sauromalus obesus*) of the American Southwest and northern Mexico.

As far as the general texture of the skin, it is somewhat akin to that of the more familiar leopard gecko (*Eublepharis macularius*) with its knobby texture. When viewing a uromastyx, however, the knobs of the scales are much smaller and closer together than those of the leopard gecko. With the scales being so close together, they form a fine network of flat circular scales on the dorsal region as well as the stomach area. These small circular scales change to enlarged spines on the legs and tail. The tail especially is covered in whorls of very dangerous-looking spines extending from the base of the tail where it meets the body to the tip. The size and sharpness of the spines varies by species, with some having spines that are no more than little bumps.

Some people describe uros as looking like

> The scales on the tails of *Uromastyx* species are enlarged and rough. In some species, the scales are sharp spikes.

It's All in the Teeth

The family Agamidae contains approximately 350 species distributed over 45 genera. Like the lizards of the family Chamaeleonidae, agamids are distinguished from the other families in their suborder by the presence of acrodont teeth, teeth that are situated at the top of the jaw bone.

some dinosaurs, given their spiked tail. However, like other lizards, they are not closely related to dinosaurs. For those having no experience with uromastyx, they may appear to be vicious carnivores with powerful limbs ending in some scary-looking claws that look as if they could be used to tear flesh from their prey. This first impression could not be farther from the truth. Uros are docile pets that many say could rival the bearded dragon (*Pogona vitticeps*) as the herp keeper's best friend. When I look at uros I sometimes think of them as tortoises without shells. Like most tortoises, uromastyx are primarily herbivorous.

While most species of *Uromastyx* are sexually dimorphic—meaning that the males and females differ in color or some other obvious characteristic—some species have occurrences of "male mimics" when it comes to coloring. These mimic females that have the same bright markings as their male counterparts and are thus easily misidentified as males. What advantage the females gain from this coloration is not known.

Natural Range

These incredible saurians are found naturally in Morocco, Algeria, Tunisia, Mauritania, Libya, Senegal, Sudan, Chad, Mali, Niger, Egypt, Eritrea, Israel, Saudi Arabia, Yemen, Oman, the United Arab Emirates, Qatar, Kuwait, Iran, Iraq, Syria, Jordan, Afghanistan, Pakistan, India, Somalia, and Djibouti. The farthest south they have been found is

southern Somalia. Uromastyx live mainly in desert areas, but there are a few species, such as *U. geryi* and *U. benti*, that occur in montane regions of Saudi Arabia and Africa. *U. geryi* is found within the Hoggar mountain range of southern Algeria; this is considered an arid mountain range with little vegetation. *U. benti* occurs in high elevations of the rocky Yemen coastline.

In the Wild

Uromastyx are thought to live in loose groups or colonies among the rocky outcroppings within their native deserts. The size of these colonies' foraging areas is reported to be at least several hectares; a hectare comprises about 2 acres (8094 square meters). All of the species inhabit very arid areas of the world. Temperatures over most of the range can exceed 125°F (51.7°C). When most people think of deserts, they have visions of blowing sand dunes and little or no vegetation. This is only somewhat true when we are speaking of the habitat of uromastyx. Many come from arid rocky habitats, and there is more vegetation present than one would think.

The clay-heavy soil types found in uromastyx habitats lend themselves to burrow excavating because such soils hold a burrow well. The uromastyx's sharp claws and powerful arms are no doubt specifically designed for digging through interspersed sand, gravel, and clay soils. Burrows have been discovered in excess of ten feet (3 m) in

Uromastyx live in arid habitats from Africa to the Middle East and western Asia.

length. Sherman A. Minton reports in his observations that *Uromastyx* species seem to have some type of homing instinct; when threatened they will run over 147 feet (45 m) to reach their particular hole.

He states that occasionally eight to ten young uromastyx will sometimes try to enter the same hole, leaving their tails flailing wildly in the air like something out of a cartoon. Minton also observed that they will also attempt to enter a burrow that is either obviously too small or occupied by another lizard, which will eject the intruder.

This herpetologist in Mauritania dug a uro out of a burrow that was several feet long.

Natural Diet

For most reptiles, information on their natural diet is sorely lacking. However, there is fairly extensive literature on the plants eaten in the wild by one species of uro. *Uromastyx aegyptia microlepis*, a subspecies of the Egyptian uromastyx, is known to consume various types of plants found in its native environment. These include *Aerva javanica* (cockscomb family), *Citrullus colocynthis* (gourd family), *Haloxylon salicornicum* (goosefoot family), *Heliotropium kotschyi* (borage family), and *Leptadenia pyrotechnica* (milkweed family) Various authors have

Native Plants

Many types of plants grow within the natural range of uromastyx. These range from *Acacia* to *Hibiscus*. Gourds, cockscombs, peas, borages, grasses, and euphorbias also are among the plants that uromastyx encounter. Acacias are harvested by the locals to be used for making charcoal, causing destruction of uromastyx habitat.

Burrows provide uros with shelter from both extreme temperatures and predators. This is a wild ocellated uromastyx near its burrow in northeastern Sudan.

documented *U. a. microlepis* eating these species of plants. These differ slightly from what one researcher found during a one-year study of this species. Researchers observed the lizards ingesting the following plants: *Moltkiopsis ciliata* (borage family), *Pennisetum divisium capitata* (grass family), *Polygala erioptera* (milkwort family), *Pulicaria glutinosa* (daisy family), *Stipagrostis plumosa* (grass family), *Taverniera cuneifolia* (legume family), *Fagonia* sp. (caltrop family), *Zygophyllum* sp. (caltrop family), *Horwoodia dicksoneae* (mustard family), and *Plantago boissieri* (plantain family). In "Notes on the Diet, Survival Rate, and Burrow Specifics of *Uromastyx aegyptia microlepis* from the United Arab Emirates," Peter Cunningham states that the coarse desert grasses were favored over the other plants that were available. The differences could be attributed to the location of the specific studies or even a difference in seasonal availability of the plants.

Behaviors

Behavioral reports on wild uromastyx are extremely limited. Uromastyx will go into their burrows head first, leaving only their spiky tails exposed. This would force any would-be predator to expose the soft interior of its mouth to the flailing spikes. However, Minton reports that uromastyx do not do this, and instead shove loose dirt up behind themselves, much as a pocket gopher does. He also saw uromastyx being preyed upon by jackals and the laggar falcon (*Falco jugger*). Desert peoples that share the area with uromastyx capture the lizards for food and for the fat reserves in their tails, which are believed to have aphrodisiac and other medicinal properties.

Uromastyx that I have worked with in captivity have been extremely ready to lash their tails violently at me during cage cleaning. They have never caused more than a scrape to the skin. I have never seen them shovel dirt behind themselves as described by Minton. This might be something they do only in nature.

The Egyptian uromastyx is the largest species in the genus, reaching a total length of up to 30 inches (76.2 cm).

It has been said that the biggest threat to uromastyx is that of local bird life. Nearly all species of raptors take lizards and snakes (sometimes outweighing the bird itself) as prey. It would also not be very hard to pick out such a brightly colored animal on the ground, given the acuity of the birds' eyesight from high up in the sky. It is also said by some researchers that this is why uromastyx choose to move about and feed at the hottest times of the day. Presumably there are fewer birds or other predators active at the height of mid-day in the specific areas predators and uros cohabit. Sometimes the raptor

The Arabian uromastyx is a sub-species of the Egyptian. It is not as commonly seen in the reptile hobby but is sometimes available.

will discard the spiky tail while eating the rest of the lizard.

It has also been reported that uromastyx in their native habitat will exhibit a behavior much like that of the chuckwalla (*Sauromalus obesus*). When threatened they will go into a rocky crevice and wedge themselves into it. Once there they will inhale deeply, effectively inflating themselves. Firmly wedged in place, they can not be removed without a serious struggle, which for most predators involves too much work. Uros that I have owned have performed the wedging-in trick, and I can attest that they are capable of remaining in such a crack for hours while apparently enduring no undue stress.

The Species

Uromastyx aegyptia

Uromastyx *aegyptia* has the honor of being the largest *Uromastyx*—up to 30 inches (76.2 cm). There are two subspecies, U. *aegyptia aegyptia*, commonly called the Egyptian uromastyx, and U. *a. microlepis*. The latter was described by Blanford in 1874 and is known as the Arabian uromastyx. Both subspecies appear in the hobby.

Given the common and specific name, you could conclude that U. *a. aegyptia* is found in Egypt and you would be correct, but it ranges over more than just Egypt. It occurs also in Libya, Israel, northern Saudi Arabia, Iraq, Iran, Syria, and Jordan. U. *a. microlepis* occurs in the Arabian Peninsula, Iran, Iraq, Syria, Jordan, and Israel. U. *a. microlepis* and U. *a. aegyptia* overlap in their home ranges according to some researchers, and this has led to much debate about whether they are subspecies or actually distinct species.

This species has the typical tan color that would be expected of most desert-dwelling reptile species. There are variations in the shading, with browns and grays often predominating. U. *a. microlepis* apparently shows a slight yellow to orange coloration near the neck, with small spots that are easily seen when the lizard is are warm. Overall, they are darker than U. *a. aegyptia* when compared side by side. Extremely small scales cover the dorsal surface in both subspecies. The scales are so fine that these lizards may appear to be scaleless at first glance. The spines on the tail are large and well developed.

Ranging from Libya to Senegal, North African uromastyx is a fitting common name for *U. acanthinura*.

Uromastyx acanthinura

In North Africa we find *U. acanthinura*, appropriately called the North African uromastyx. This species can attain lengths of 15.75 inches (40 cm). There really is no typical coloration within the nominate subspecies (*U. a. acanthinura*), as it is highly variable. The head of most North African uros is typically black in coloration, while the body has a netlike or honeycomb pattern of yellow, gray, red, and green. There are three subspecies, although the taxonomy of this species is confusing; many herpetologists do not recognize any subspecies.

U. a. acanthinura occurs in Libya, Senegal, Algeria, Tunisia, Morocco, and the northern part of the Western Sahara. In these areas, it lives on the rocky slopes of mountain valleys and even in cultivated land areas, but the humidity is always low in their habitat.

There are evidently two other subspecies recognized, *U. a. nigerrima* and *U. a. werneri*. *U. a. nigerrima* was described for the first time in 1913 by Hartert and is found in southwestern Algeria. *U. a. werneri* is found in Morocco and Algeria. These two subspecies are poorly known and hard to distinguish from each other and *U. a. acanthinura*. Until recently, herpetologists considered *U. dispar flavifasciata* a subspecies of *U. acanthinura*.

Uromastyx alfredschmidti

Uromastyx alfredschmidti occurs exclusively in the areas of Tassili Ajjer in Algeria. U.

alfredschmidti is known as the ebony uromastyx, and males are totally black. The females may have various white irregular blotches on the head and tail. *U. alfredschmidti* ranges from about 13 to 16 inches (33 to 40.6 cm) in total length.

Ebony uromastyx inhabit the same type of rocky desert outcroppings that seemingly all uros call home. They feed on species of *Artemisia*, a genus that includes wormwood, mugwort, and tarragon. However, they do not seem to feed on these plants exclusively.

The ebony uromastyx is similar in appearance to a few other species. In order to tell the difference between *U. alfredschmidti* and *U. acanthinura*, you must look at the tail. The tails of both *U. geryi* and *U. alfredschmidti* are long and tapering, while the tail of *U. acanthinura* is squat and broad. The difference is very obvious. In comparing *U. geryi* and *U. alfredschmidti*, note that *U. geryi* is smaller and more brightly colored than *U. alfredschmidti*.

There do not seem to be any pure *U. alfredschmidti* in the herp hobby. There are some individuals in the hobby that seem to be crossbreeds of *U. alfredschmidti* and *U. dispar flavifasciata*. *U. afredschmidti* has not knowingly been imported, although it is possible it has been brought into the US or Europe under an incorrect name.

Uromastyx dispar

The Sudanese uromastyx, *U. dispar*, was originally described as a subspecies of *U. acanthinura* by Heyden in 1827. Wilms and Böhme reexamined the genus in 2001 and elevated *U. dispar* to full species status, based on their phylogenetic research. Wilms and Böhme state that *U. maliensis*, which was originally considered a separate species, is actually a subspecies of *U.*

The Name Game

There have been a number of taxonomic changes within *Uromastyx* over the years. Some recent changes concern *U. acanthinura*. Wilms and Böhme described two new species in 2001, *U. alfredschmidti* and *U. dispar*. *U. dispar* was actually described in 1827 by Heyden, but it was long considered a subspecies of *U. acanthinura*. Some authorities still consider both of these new species to be subspecies of *U. acanthinura*. However, according to the Convention on International Trade in Endangered Species (C.I.T.E.S), *Uromastyx dispar* and *Uromastyx alfredschmidti* should be accepted as true species.

dispar. So now we have *U. dispar dispar*, *U. dispar maliensis*, and *U. dispar flavifasciata*. *U. d. maliensis*—usually called the Mali uromastyx in the hobby—is a brown color with a lighter yellow herringbone pattern. Males that are healthy and warm are often bright yellow with black heads and limbs; the yellow color sometimes obscures the herringbone pattern.

Of the subspecies of *Uromastyx dispar*, only the Mali uromastyx is common in the pet trade.

   U. d. flavifasciata was first described by Mertens in 1962, although it was originally considered a subspecies of *U. acanthinura*. This particular subspecies is a dark lizard with bright solid (usually white) barring in a herringbone pattern like that of *U. d. maliensis*. Adult males are usually striped almost like a reverse zebra with very bold white stripes over a dark black background. The females on the other hand are usually a tan ground color with small white spots running horizontally across the back in distinct lines. This uro lives in Senegal, Mauritania, and southern Morocco.

   The belly striping in adults is much higher in *U. d. flavifasciata* than it is in *U. d. maliensis*. Generally speaking, both subspecies attain a size 13 to 16 inches (33 to 40.6 cm) in males and only slightly smaller than that in females. The two subspecies will interbreed with each other; a cross between two different subspecies of the same species is called an *intergrade*. Both subspecies seem to overlap ranges in Niger, Egypt, Mali, and Sudan.

Uromastyx geryi

   Uromastyx geryi, the Niger Uromastyx

Aggressive North African Species

The North African uromastyx has a reputation for being a somewhat aggressive and flighty species. In my experience, I have never encountered one that could not be tamed with regular handling.

(sometimes called the Saharan uromastyx) is found in southern Algeria, Mali, and Niger in the Aïr Mountains, which are north of Agadez and east of Arlit. They also occur in the Hoggar Mountains of Algeria, which are located southeast of Adrar. This particular species ranges in size from 11 to 14 inches (27.9 to 35.6 cm) when fully grown. U. geyri is differentiated from U. acanthinura by the number of whorl scales present on the tail: U. geryi has 20 to 24 whorls, while U. acanthinura has 17 to 20.

Three color varieties appear in the hobby: red, orange, and yellow. Males are considerably brighter than females. All of the colors are brightest and densest on the dorsal region. The ventral surface is pale cream, with only a hint of the dorsal color, although some individuals have brightly colored bellies. The females are tan to brown, with faint traces of the red, orange, or yellow of their male counterparts.

Morph Mistakes

There are three separate color morphs of *U. benti*. They are the orange, the red, and the rainbow (sometimes called the mountain benti). The rainbow benti is sometimes mistakenly sold as *U. ocellata philbyi*. It is very easy to see that *U. o. philbyi* is different from *U. benti* because *U. o. philbyi* exhibits a row of enlarged femoral pores. *U. benti* lacks femoral pores.

Uromastyx benti

Uromastyx benti is called the rainbow uromastyx, but it is also referred to as Bent's spiny-tailed lizard or mountain benti. It occurs on the coast of Yemen and in Saudi Arabia and is fairlyy common in Oman as well. Its rocky habitat does not allow for agriculture, and therefore the human population density is low, which in turn means less habitat destruction. According to C.I.T.E.S and several studies, the destruction of habitat—mainly removal of

The Saharan uromastyx is native to the arid mountains of Niger, Mali, and Algeria. This is the yellow form.

acacia trees to make charcoal—is a large threat to some *Uromastyx* species, but this is not a major issue for *U. benti*.

Males of *U. benti* have a bluish torso with white spots that bleed into a reddish color towards the posterior of the lizard. The females are typically tan in color while having a reddish tail. They obtain an overall length of approximately 12 inches (30.5 cm). *U. benti* is easy to recognize because it is the only species (aside from the rare *U. princeps*) that lacks femoral and pre-anal pores. The tail tapers strongly and makes up over half the total length of the animal.

It is reported that *U. benti* also enjoys branches for climbing. This behavior is unique within the genus. Most other species prefer to stay on the ground within reach of a burrow or crevice, but *U. benti* seems happy crawling over and basking on branches.

Uromastyx hardwickii

Uromastyx hardwickii, the Indian uromastyx, is a mountain-dwelling species occurring in the northwest portion of India and ranging into Pakistan. *U. hardwickii* typically obtains a length of about 18 inches (45.7 cm). The coloration for this species is usually grayish tan with light yellow spotting. However, individuals may also appear with some dark spots or a fine mesh of interconnected lines, which are typically a darker brown color than the ground color. The belly of this particular species is usually white, with a blue-black spot on the inner thigh of each hindlimb.

U. benti basking in the wild. Based on the coloration, this is probably a female.

The Indian uromastyx often lives in large colonies within its home range of Pakistan, Afghanistan, and India.

This peculiarity is also seen on the side-blotched lizard (*Uta stansburiana*) found in the western United States, which has a small dark spot where the forelimb meets the body. The tail in *U. hardwickii* is less spiny than is common in other uros. The spines are small and not very pronounced. There are more rows of spines separated by larger spaces than in other species.

Uromastyx ocellata

This species has two subspecies, *U. ocellata ocellata* and *U. ocellata philbyi*. Whether they are subspecies or separate species is a matter of some debate. Wilms and Böhme consider *philbyi* a subspecies of *U. ocellata*, and that taxonomy is followed here. *Uromastyx ocellata ocellata*, the ocellated or Sudanese uromastyx, occurs in northwestern Somalia, Djibouti, Eritrea, northern Sudan, and southeastern Egypt. It is typically found in the wadis (gullies or riverbeds that are only wet during the rainy season) and mountainous rocky desert areas where it has access to the acacias on which it feeds. It will sometimes retreat to the boulders or may burrow into the wadis themselves.

U. ocellata is very closely related to *U. ornata* and is sometimes considered a subspecies.

Close Relatives

Several uromastyx are closely related to *U. ornata* and *U. ocellata*. These are commonly called the ornata group or ornate group. The species in this group are *U. ornata, U. ocellata, U. benti, U. macfadyeni,* and probably the recently described *U. yemenensis*. These species can be difficult to tell apart, and their relationships are not fully understood.

These two species are difficult to tell apart. U. ocellata does not have notched or scalloped scales at the front edge of the ear, while U. ornata does have these scales.

U. ocellata can reach lengths of up to 14 inches (35.6 cm).

There are quite a number of color morphs of ocellated uromastyx. I have personally seen high-orange, tan and white, and high-blue morphs. The high orange literally looked as if it rolled around in the dust from puffed cheese snacks. The high-blue morph is the color of a clear blue summer sky. The tan and white morph appears as if someone had taken the lizard and dipped its tail into white paint and then flicked the paintbrush onto its body, leaving a tan lizard with a white tail and bright white spots.

U. ocellata philbyi occurs in western Saudi Arabia and northwest Yemen. It is often called the Yemeni uromastyx. Adults of this species reach about 12 inches (30.5) in length and have a more evenly reticulated pattern than seen in U. ornata. It also has a broader tail than U. ornata and U. ocellata ocellata.

The status of U. ocellata philbyi is confusing. This results from the fact that to the knowledge of most professional breeders, there has never been a U. o. philbyi individual kept or bred in captivity. This also goes without mentioning that there are no existing records of any ever being imported into the United States. However, there are breeders who say they are producing U. o. philbyi. It is entirely possible that some U. o. philbyi were imported as another species or subspecies—most likely either U. ocellata ocellata or U. benti. If you are interested in obtaining U. o. philbyi, make sure you are actually getting U. o. philbyi and not some other uromastyx.

Uromastyx ornata

Uromastyx ornata, the ornate uromastyx, occurs in eastern Egypt, Israel, and Saudi Arabia. It typically reaches a total length of 12 inches (30.5 cm), with the tail making up about half that length. The scales bordering the front of the ear opening are toothed, a trait that distinguishes this species from U. ocellata.

U. ornata is sexually dichromatic, meaning that the females and males are easily identified by their coloration. The males have heads colored in combinations of green, blue, and rust. These colors are repeated in the various-sized bands that appear on the bodies of these animals. The base color for most males is a sky blue to deep cobalt blue or a bright green. Whether they are blue or green, they will have large yellow spots broken up by black or gray reticulations.

The Yemeni uromastyx occurs in extreme southwestern Saudi Arabia and in Yemen.

Females are usually light brown or tan, with hints of the blues and greens. On females, the yellow spots are present but faint. Males typically do not show the full coloration until sexual maturity is reached—usually around three years of age. Both males and females have seven distinct bands on the back running across the width of the body. Within these bands, there are yellow spots encircled by a rust or brown color. Between the bands there are brown scribble-like markings.

Uromastyx macfadyeni

This species is considered part of the ornata group (along with ornata, ocellata, and benti,) and formerly was considered a subspecies of ocellata. It was originally described by Parker in 1932. It is usually called the Somali uromastyx. It is only sporadically imported and rarely available. Those who do import this species rarely sell them to someone who doesn't have a track record of breeding other Uromastyx. Wild-caught Somali uros are difficult to acclimate. These are shy lizards.

U. macfadyeni is comparable to U. ocellata in color, but the pattern on the dorsum differs slightly. This pattern is a well-defined rib-bone pattern, i.e., a central line running down the backbone with straight bars of color coming off this line. Males have yellow spots surrounded by a sandy tan color. Both males and females have a dark blue ground color; this may be very covered and broken by the yellow spots and brown reticulations. Juveniles are a mottled brown, and while they show the pattern, it becomes more evident as they grow. This species does not exceed 10 ten inches (25.4 cm) in length. The spines on the sides of the tail are longer than in the other species within the ornate group.

Other Species

There are seven other species of *Uromastyx*, but little information on captive individuals or conditions in the wild is available. There are two closely related species, *U. asmussi* and *U. loricata*. They are very similar in appearance and have natural ranges that possibly overlap. *U. asmussi* (the Iranian spiny-tail) as described by Strauch in 1863 is cited as occurring from western Iran across Afghanistan and into Pakistan. It is larger—sometimes over 20 inches (50.8 cm) in total length—and more colorful than *U. hardwickii*, as well as having larger and heavier caudal spines. It is also has spiny tubercles on the dorsum; these turbercles may be red in males. *U. loricata* (the Iraqi spiny-tail) was described by Blanford in 1874. This is a pale species that is yellowish to reddish when warm. It may have brown to yellow spots. Unlike *U. asmussi*, the scales in front of the ear are smooth, not scalloped.

Uromastyx leptieni occurs in the United Arab Emirates and possibly Oman. Adults are difficult to distinguish from *U. aegyptia microlepis* (which occurs in the same area), but the juveniles are easy to tell apart. Young *U. leptieni* are reddish brown, with fine dark brown flecks, and *microlepis* is a grayish brown, with yellow bands and sometimes reddish spots. Adult *U. leptieni* have tubercles running from the pelvic area up to the front legs, which *microplepis* lacks.

Uromatyx occidentalis was described by Mateo, Geniez, Lopez-Jurado, and Bons in 1999. The few available photos of this animal show a gray and brown mottled lizard having a pale green wash over the sides that gets brighter on the forelimbs and chin. The snout is short

Mmm...Flowers

According to Douglas Dix of Deerfern Farms, one of the two main foods of *U. o. ornata* is the umbrella thorn acacia (*Acacia tortilis*), of which it eats mostly the blooms. Hibiscus is the other major food. (personal comm.).

Ornate uromastyx are found in Egypt, Israel, and Saudi Arabia, where they feed mainly on acacia and hibiscus.

and stubby. It has enlarged spiny scales on the hind legs. It is found in Western Sahara.

Uromastyx yemenensis was described in 2007 by Wilms and Schmitz. It is closely related to *U. benti* and occurs in extreme southwestern Arabia. There are two subspecies, *U. y. yemenensis* and *U. y. shobraki*. It has smaller scales than *U. benti* but is otherwise similar.

There are two short-tailed uromastyx that look quite different from the rest of the genus. *U. princeps* was described by O'Shaughnessy 1880 and is known as the armored uromastyx. *U. thomasi* was described by Parker 1932 and is known commonly as the Omani spiny tail. Both species have rounded, almost disk-like tails that are roughly half the entire length of the animal itself. *U. princeps* has long tail spines that are very high and sharp when compared to those of other uros. *U. thomasi*, on the other hand, has very low spines on the tail. *U. princeps* is found in Somalia and other areas on the Horn of Africa. It is a small species, rarely reaching 9 inches (22.9 cm) in total length. It is olive brown turning to rust near the spine and has some brown spots. *U. thomasi* ranges from 6 to 8 inches (15.2 to 20.3 cm) long. When warm, this species is greenish gray to pale blue, with a diffuse reddish stripe running down the back. *U. thomasi* appears to be restricted to Oman, including Masirah Island.

Chapter 2

Uromastyx as Pets

It is always been my sincerest belief that before you buy any reptile or amphibian you should first do your homework. This means reading everything you can get your hands on regarding the species you want to keep. Not only will this save you a lot of trouble—money, veterinary care, frustration—but it will also save your new pet from the possibility of a horrible death. By understanding the needs of the animal you desire and preparing for its arrival, you can avoid this scenario. Both you and your pet will be happier and healthier for it.

The Unpleasant Facts

Each year hundreds, if not thousands, of reptiles are purchased and then abandoned or neglected. They are made to live in cramped cages, often with improper lighting and heating, causing them to be unhealthy and suffering. This can be attributed to several factors. Most assuredly, the leading factor in the ill health of all reptiles is caused by the mass importation of wild-caught animals at cheap prices. Because they are so inexpensive and common, they often are thought of as disposable pets.

Fortunately, uromastyx are usually not a buy-and-ditch pet. They are typically more expensive than other popular lizards, such as bearded dragons (*Pogona vitticeps*) and green iguanas (*Iguana iguana*). This is because there are still very few breeders who can produce them in captivity on a routine basis. In recent years, however, more uros have been imported, so prices for some varieties are dropping. This could lead to more of them suffering an unpleasant fate.

Make sure you understand the care a uromastyx needs before you purchase one. This is a hatchling ornate uromastyx.

Another huge reason that reptiles are abandoned is lack of understanding of the herps' requirements. I have seen many new hobbyists with sickly reptiles who say that the person who sold it to them gave them no or little information. Granted that responsible sellers will discuss a herp's care before selling it, it is still the buyer's responsibility to ask questions and obtain all of the information needed to ensure a healthy life for the animal. Too many new hobbyists obtain a herp before knowing how to care for it, and then find out that the proper care entails more expense or time than they are willing to provide. The end result is either a herp that receives substandard care and consequently lives a shortened, miserable life or a herp that is given over to a different owner or animal shelter.

Where to Buy a Uromastyx

You can obtain a uromastyx from a number of different sources. There are pros and cons to each one.

Depending on where you live, some sources will be more or less convenient or costly. This section only discusses the sources themselves; the following section talks about how to pick out a healthy uro.

Before you actually buy a uromastyx, it is important to know if you need a permit to keep reptiles or other exotic animals in your location. This is common in many states and municipalities. Your local pet store should be able to provide you with this information, as will an Internet search.

Wild-Caught versus Captive-Bred

One of the first things a prospective keeper should understand is the difference between wild-caught and captive-bred animals. At first this may seem as if the animals in these two different groups are easy to distinguish, but you will find it can be difficult at times. The two terms refer to the source of the individual animal in question. As you probably would guess, wild-caught herps are captured in nature and shipped out to various live animal dealers. Captive-bred herps have hatched out of eggs laid by parents who mated in captivity.

Wild-caught animals are normally caught in their native countries and then exported to their place of sale, all the while enduring days and sometimes weeks under very poor conditions. To say the least, this makes for an extremely stressful trip. They will usually be loaded with all types of parasites, both internal and external, and probably suffering from dehydration and exposure to improper temperatures. So besides what you have paid for the animal already, you must now go to the vet and have the lizard examined and treated for any of host of health issues. When produced in captivity, uros (and herps in general) tend to be in better overall health and for this reason are much more desirable.

Unfortunately, uromastyx are not bred in captivity in large enough numbers to fulfill the

Time Commitment

When I am asked to rate the care of a species, I usually do this in terms of the hours spent taking care of the animal. Owning any uromastyx will consume roughly about an hour a day and then approximately seven to eight hours a week; this includes disinfection and routine cage maintenance. In Chapter 3 there is a thorough overview of daily, weekly, and monthly tasks in the maintenance of all uromastyx.

Wild-caught animals are often shipped and held in overcrowded and stressful conditions as these freshly imported *U. benti* are.

demand for these docile and interesting lizards. They are still heavily collected from the wild to supply the pet trade. When acquiring a wild-caught uromastyx, it is especially important to carefully examine it for any possible health problems. You should also find out how long it has been in captivity. Those that have been in captivity for an extended time are usually less likely to do poorly than those that have just arrived at the pet store or other dealer.

Breeders

I personally recommend buying your uromastyx from a reputable breeder over other sources. It is easy to find a reputable breeder by simply asking the local herpetological society or by going online and searching various reptile forums. When you find a breeder, ask for references from previous customers. Any breeder who has invested the time and money will be happy to give these to you.

Reputable breeders, whether you meet them via the Internet or through a local reptile enthusiast, will not only guarantee live arrival (if the animal is being shipped to you) but also offer some type of warranty, such as replacing or refunding your money if the uro dies within a month or something similar. Typically, just by visiting their personal website and exchanging e-mails you can get a feel for who is and isn't professional. Again, if you have doubts, talk to people who have purchased there before, ask about the breeder in online herp forums, or just simply go to another breeder.

Herp Expos

Herp expos (also called herp shows, reptile expos, and reptile shows) are another place to pick up your new pet. These are semi-regular events held in convention centers and the like. At a herp expo, breeders and other vendors come to sell herps, food, enclosures, supplies, and other herp-related items. They can range in size from just a few tables in a school gymnasium to hundreds of tables taking up an entire convention center. At herp expos the prices often are very good, and there is a wide selection of animals to choose from, including color morphs and rare species.

At a herp expo, you are again advised to buy from a reputable dealer. When you attend

Life Span

Uromastyx are known to live approximately 15 to 20 years if they are cared for properly. Life spans longer than 20 years are not unheard of. As we learn more about the needs of these lizards and improve our abilities to provide for those needs, captive life spans may increase.

I Found One!

A young woman came into the shop where I worked and stated to me that she had found a uromastyx wandering the streets of her local neighborhood. Being skeptical about such windfalls, I asked her how this occurred. She explained that while driving she saw this lizard creature wandering the street. She had taken it to the local vet to have it examined and the vet told her what it was and how to care for it. I still doubted that it was a uro. I therefore asked her to bring it in so I could see it for myself. She in turn brought in a large Egyptian uro, *Uromastyx aegyptia*. She said she had posted signs throughout the neighborhood, but no one claimed the lizard. I guess this goes to show that some folks are just lucky—and others are just plain careless.

What Do Those Letters Stand for?

Vendors at herp expos usually display their animals in deli cups or other small enclosures. The labels on the deli cups will often have abbreviations on them, such as W/C or C/B. W/C means the animals is wild-caught and C/B should mean captive-bred. However, this is where some people in the industry take liberties with interpretations. Occasionally the C/B may mean captive-born. Captive-born means the mother was wild- caught while carrying fertilized eggs, which she laid in captivity. The more accurate term for this situation is captive-hatched, but not every vendor uses that term.

one of these events, you will find yourself among a throng of breeders and dealers. For the most part, all of the people you meet will be friendly and honest. Nevertheless, as in any other industry, there are those who just want to make money. More often than not, you will want to buy a baby rather than an adult unless you are interested in breeding; this is something that will be covered in later chapters.

Finding yourself at the show, you will no doubt see countless lines of deli cups and other types of displays with lights above to show off the animals' colors. Occasionally you will be lucky enough to see the parents of the offspring so that you might see what the results might be as the babies grow up. The only drawback is that because of the busy surroundings and the stress of traveling to the show, uromastyx might not be in the best color and might not eat if offered food. As long as you buy from a reputable vendor and get a business card or other contact information, you should feel secure about your purchase.

Pet Stores

Pet stores are another location where you can occasionally find uromastyx for sale. Even the pet superstores stock them once in a while. It is not rare to see locally owned "mom and pop" pet shops selling the more common species. Once again, unless you have experience with buying other pets from the store, ask a lot of questions. The sales people should have no problem answering them. I would be sure to inquire as to where the animals came from, as well as how long they had been in the store, etc. Additionally, check around the store to see if its personnel are offering appropriate care to the other livestock. If other animals are poorly cared for, there is a good chance the uros are as well.

Occasionally, if a particular animal has been in the store for an extended period of time and has not sold there might be a possibility of obtaining that particular one at a much reduced rate. Be sure to inquire in depth, however, as to why the animal has not been sold yet. You wouldn't want to make the purchase only to discover that your new pet has some medical or behavioral issue that wasn't disclosed.

Adoption

Adoption is another option, although uromastyx are rarely put up for adoption. Usually this happens when the lizards' humans are moving, divorcing, etc. The keeper will not be able to keep the lizard and simply wants it to go to a good home and therefore is willing to give it up for adoption, typically with the cage and all accessories included. Check your local paper, animal shelter, and herp society to see whether this is an option in your area. You may also be able to find a uromastyx for adoption through online herp forums.

Ornate uromastyx (baby white phase ones shown here) probably are the most frequently captive-bred species, although no uro is commonly bred.

Selecting a Healthy Uromastyx

Starting with a healthy uromastyx is critical. If you start with an animal that is unhealthy, you will end up spending a lot of time and money trying to make it well—with only a very small chance of success. Before you go shopping for one, you need to learn what a healthy uromastyx looks like and how it behaves.

Feeding

It is always a good idea to ask whether it is possible to see the animal feed. This may be impossible at a herp expo, but it is

Watch the Lizard

If you are buying your uro from a pet store, it's a good idea to observe it on a few separate occasions. This allows you to spot any behaviors that might alert you to an ailment or injury. I have never had problems with a reptile I purchased when I have seen that animal feed and observed it on a few random occasions.

otherwise a good practice. If the shopkeeper is unwilling, you should probably take your business elsewhere. However, it is not always appropriate to have uros "feed on command," so to speak. In such cases, ask the shopkeeper when they typically feed and come back then. At this time, inquire about the current diet the vendor feeds the uro. This does two things: it allows you to stock the same diet and lets you know whether the vendor is supplying proper care.

Closer Inspection

After the uromastyx has fed, ask to hold it. You should handle any uromastyx you plan to buy, as this gives you an opportunity to look closely for health issues. The lizard should exhibit interest via tongue flicking and possibly trying to escape. It may wriggle or lash its tail while it is in your grasp.

While holding the uromastyx, you should look for one that is plump, with taut skin over the entire body, although wrinkles along the sides are normal. Uromastyx are typically wrinkled somewhat at what I have come to know as the midline, which is the halfway point when moving from the spine horizontally towards the belly. In this region, they have slight skin folds, somewhat along the lines of the folds on an elderly person.

The body itself should be free of any lumps, scars, or any other disfigurements. The spine should be straight and not kinked in any way. The eyes should be clear and free of any mucous material, and they should also not be watering to the extent where it may look as if the uro is tearing up and ready to cry.

The body should also be free of any ticks and or mites, external parasites often found on lizards, especially wild-caught lizards. Mites are very small and somewhat hard to see. They will appear much like crawling flecks of pepper. Ticks are larger and are almost a sure sign you are dealing with a wild-caught animal. It is best to avoid purchasing uromastyx that have either mites or ticks.

If at all possible view the lizard head on and look carefully at the mouth area. Make sure the jaws are not deformed and that there is no dried crust in the mouth area. You may see some whitish crust in or around the nostril area, but this is not any cause for alarm. This is a completely normal condition in which the uro is expelling extra salts through its nose. This type of behavior is commonly seen in green iguanas as well. Any crystal or crust formation about the lips and or mouth area may mean that the lizard either has or has recently overcome a respiratory infection. It is best to avoid these animals.

There is, however, an ailment that generally afflicts only Uromastyx acanthinura. It is an infection that appears as a crusty formation around the lips of the uro. It is specifically different from the disease typically called mouth rot and cannot be treated the same way. The specifics of this and other diseases and ailments are discussed in later chapters. If you are looking at a U. acanthinura specimen and it has crusty lips, do not purchase it.

Before you purchase a uromastyx, inspect it closely for signs of ill health. This is a young Indian uromastyx.

Lastly, gently turn the lizard upside down while in your hand. The uro should struggle against this, which is a good sign. Look at the vent or cloaca, making sure that it is free of any protrusions, crust, and mucus—all signs of illness.

With all this inspection and handling, you will be able to get a feel for the uro's specific personality. These lizards definitely have a personality, which you will be able to determine during this cursory inspection period.

Bringing it Home

Now you have found a healthy lizard that you think would make a great pet, and you're ready to bring it home…or are you? In all the years that I have been in the herpetological industry, I have seen maybe a handful of people who were actually "ready" to bring home their new pets. Before bringing home any new pet, you should always have its enclosure set up with all the elements in place. This includes the lighting and heating, which should both be working and be within the prescribed ranges for at least a full day. This will enable a much less stressful transfer process for the uromastyx from the pet store to its new home.

There are many different methods for transporting lizards from a shop or expo to your home. Following are some guidelines for a low-stress and safe journey. Make sure that the reptile is in complete darkness. That being said, uromastyx often are transported in cloth bags. I never recommend transporting uromastyx in cloth bags, because they may become entangled within the loose strings and severely injure a toe or claw. I always use a cardboard box whenever I transport lizards of any kind. This way I am able to enclose them in complete darkness and don't have to worry about the lizards catching a toe or claw and injuring themselves.

> A uromastyx that has closed or sunken eyes is likely to be unhealthy and should not be purchased.

Hygiene

My family and I wash our hands before and after handling any of our reptiles. Not only does this keep disease or pests from being passed around between our herps, but it's also just general good hygiene for humans. Any food preparation or cleaning of reptile-related materials is done in our bathtub or at least away from our personal eating and food preparation areas. Immediately following, we spray the tub with a pre-mixed solution of bleach and water to disinfect the area.

Quarantine

If you own any other species of reptile or amphibian within your home, I don't think it is possible to stress enough the importance of quarantining a new reptile or amphibian. For those new to the hobby this may sound a bit strange. The practice of quarantining simply means to keep the new herp separate from the herps you already have to prevent introducing any parasites or infections to your established animals. The quarantined uro will be in its own cage, and preferably it will be in a different room from any other herps you have.

During the quarantine, you will provide the newly acquired pet with adequate but minimal housing and décor, and you make sure the furnishings have been disinfected before adding them to the quarantine cage. Perform all routine maintenance, such as feeding, watering, and cleaning, on all your established and healthy animals first. Then, and only then, perform these tasks for the newly acquired reptile. These practices will ensure that if the new uro has brought an unseen pathogen it will not be spread to the other reptiles or amphibians through proximity or your contact with the infected reptile.

Quarantine should last at least one month; longer is not a bad idea. At a minimum, give the new reptile at least two weeks in which nothing is done other than the absolute necessities of maintenance such as feeding and watering. Once again, do this only after you work with the established animals. This means no handling or any other interaction with the new animal. After the quarantine time you may begin to handle the new reptile for a few minutes at a time approximately every other day, making sure to wash your hands before and after any contact with the quarantine enclosure.

Set up a new uro by itself in a quarantine enclosure. The furnishings in quarantine should be minimal but adequate for the lizard.

Handling Uromastyx

I handle all of my reptiles on a daily or every other day basis. This is a personal preference and not a requirement for any species. It is my belief that the reptiles view the interaction not only as pleasant in itself but also as a break from the monotony of the enclosure. I know of bearded dragons that have "reverted" to their wilder ways of threat postures and snapping after little more than three months had passed when they were not handled regularly. While I have never heard reports or read any documentation that uros would exhibit similar behaviors, I do believe that they would also "revert" to a more natural state of behavior when not handled on a regular basis. If you just want your uromastyx for breeding or to be beautiful and interesting display animals, you will not need to acclimate them to handling.

Flight Response

Most of the uromastyx have a strong flight response. This means that when approached they will typically flee. This is most likely a predator-aversion tactic, given that uros are small and on the menu of many other animals . When

Most uros adapt quite well to handling. This 15-year-old male ornate is quite tame.

approached the uro will typically look quickly at the approaching subject and dart for its hiding place, often referred to simply as its "hide." Then again, some uros have no qualms about being touched and handled. Some uros take greens from their human companions' hands.

In order to overcome the flight response of your uromastyx, you must first understand that the lizard has no real way of knowing you are not a predator intent on eating it. Therefore, you should take every precaution to not overly stress your new pet. It can take a month or more before the uro finally understands that you are not going to try to harm it.

Getting Started

The newly acquired uro should be allowed at least three to four days to acclimate to its new environment without being disturbed. After this period, you can approach slowly and watch the reactions of the uro. If it is still running for cover every time you approach, you can begin by touching it gently while it remains in its hide, if possible. If this is impossible due to the type of hide you are using, you are in for a longer process.

Spend time waiting and watching for the uro to come out of the hide. Sit quietly and avoid sudden motions. When the uro comes out and is eating, slowly reach into the enclosure and gently touch the uro around the dorsal area. Avoid touching the head; this is a sensitive area, and trying to touch the lizard's head will cause stress and possibly a flight response. By gently touching the back while the uro eats, it will gradually associate the hand with a positive experience. You may have to try this numerous times before the uro allows you touch it.

Forced Handling

If the uro continues to refuse to be touched it while it is eating, you can resort to

Bad Boys

I have encountered the occasional uro—typically a dominant male—that will stand its ground. It usually stands tall on its forelimbs as the threat approaches and puffs out its mid-body area. This is an attempt to look larger than it really is and hopefully bluff the approaching threat into thinking it is not worth the effort to try to eat this particular lizard.

Sometimes the threat posture will last as long as the threat is approaching. On other occasions it occurs well after the threat has actually come into contact with the uro, and the lizard does not flee until it is actually touched.

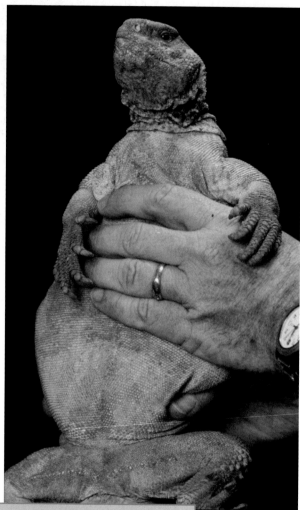

When handling a uro, it is important to support as much of its body as possible, especially when dealing with a large species such as the Egyptian.

another method, one that I call "forced handling." Before attempting forced handling, you should give the animals several weeks of refusing handling. In my opinion, forced handling is extremely stressful for reptiles, and I would generally not recommend it for anyone who has not had experience with reptiles previously. Essentially, you are going to force the uro to be handled, and it will almost definitely put up a fight against this, sometimes quite a significant fight.

Begin by trying to touch the lizard while it is eating. The uro will then run into its hide once again. After it has rested for approximately ten minutes, pull away the hide and pick up the uro as gently as possible while supporting its ventral side with the bottom of one palm. The other hand is placed palm down over the back, with the forefinger and middle finger on either side of the head—be careful to avoid choking your pet. Keep the uro pressed firmly but gently between your palms for about five minutes or so. After the uro has stopped struggling, gently stroke its dorsum with the palm, removing the two fingers from around the neck area. Uromastyx will typically stop struggling after about a minute.

Immediately place the uro back into the enclosure after a five-minute period. Repeat this

Other Pets

When keeping any type of reptiles with other pets such as dogs, cats, ferrets, and large birds we must be aware of the dangers and stresses that can be delivered to the uro by those animals. For example, large birds that are allowed to roam free may frighten uros because one of the uro's natural predators in the wild are raptors, such as the laggar falcon. Also, dogs and cats are much larger than uros and can do them serious harm should they ever come in contact. Remember that most common mammalian pets are predators, and a uromastyx is just the right size for a meal.

procedure for approximately a week. As the uro becomes more used to the procedure, you can gradually increase the amount of time that it is required to spend in this position. In my experience, this process of forced handling takes about a month or sometimes longer in order for the uro to understand that you mean it no harm.

Handling Technique

In normal cases, you can handle a uro just as you would any similarly sized lizard, such as a bearded dragon. Reach into the enclosure and touch the uro to let it know you are there and then gently scoop it up, making sure to support as much of its body as possible. Once it's out of the enclosure, make sure you support all four limbs so that the uro is comfortable. Your handling sessions can last as long as the uro is willing, in other words until it starts squirming and trying to escape. Typically, uros can be handled for about 20 to 30 minutes when acclimated. It's best not to allow a uromastyx to ride on your shoulder, as it may become nervous being so high up off the ground or fall off and injure itself.

Chapter 3

Housing

W hen it comes to housing uromastyx, there are
many opinions as to what works and what
doesn't.. We'll start by discussing the available
options for housing uros, after which. I will
explain how I personally set up my own
enclosures and explain the reasons behind my
methods. Keep in mind that while the methods and
materials presented here have worked for numerous
uromastyx keepers and breeders, they are not
necessarily the only ones that work. There is still
plenty of room to experiment and discover even
better ways to keep uros healthy.

Enclosures

First and foremost, any enclosure you select must be able to withstand extremely high heat and extremely low humidity. This does somewhat limit the materials you can use.

Enclosure Materials

Glass aquaria (both fish tanks and those made specifically for reptiles) probably are the most frequently used enclosures for uromastyx. They hold heat well and—if you use a screen top—provide good ventilation, which will keep the humidity down. The drawbacks to glass aquaria are their fragility and the price of ones large enough to house adult uromastyx.

There are Plexiglas herp enclosures available, and some handy hobbyists make cages out of this material. While Plexiglas works for many other herps, it is not the best material for uromastyx. Plexiglas is easily scratched by the abrasive sand most keepers use as a substrate, as well as by the uros' sharp claws. Plexiglas is more likely to give or expand when used, warping over time under the weight of the sand substrate. Both Plexiglas and glass aquaria can be purchased at most well-stocked pet stores.

Livestock water tanks (also called watering troughs) can be used to house uros as well. Space allowances within apartments and most homes today do not allow a livestock trough to be placed conveniently. For breeding purposes, the troughs work extremely well and are definitely more economical than trying to set up four or five terraria of the required size for a breeding colony. It is also very easy to monitor the behaviors of the uros. The only clear disadvantages to using water troughs is their size and their somewhat unsightly appearance. When using the water troughs for uros, most breeders house them in trios of one male and two females. More than that will be crowded in a trough.

There also are preformed

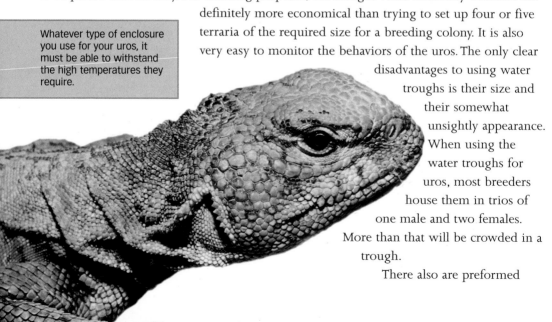

Whatever type of enclosure you use for your uros, it must be able to withstand the high temperatures they require.

plastic cages designed specifically for herps. They generally have sliding glass or Plexiglas doors on the front and holes for lighting on the top. Most of these enclosures are too small to house uromastyx. They are also more expensive than a similarly sized glass aquarium.

If you are skilled at woodworking or feel you can follow directions, there are a few websites that explain how to build enclosures. When building a cage, keep in mind it must be able to retain heat while not allowing humidity to build up.

Enclosure Size

Most reading materials on lizard care suggest that minimum cage sizes be based on the lizard's size. According to one source (www.kingsnake.com/uromastyx/urocaresheet.html), a single uro between 3 and 6 inches (7.6 and 15.2 cm) should have a tank size of 20 gallons (75.8 liters). They also recommend that for every additional 2 ¾ inches (7 cm) of length of the uro, the tank's size should double. I recommend an enclosure length of 60 or more inches (152.4 cm) for most species of uro. Some keepers recommend no less than a 55-gallon glass (208.2-l) terrarium to house *U. d. maliensis* or similarly sized species.

When housing lizards, a good rule to use is that the length of the terrarium should be five times the length of the lizard at adult size and that the width of the terrarium should be three times the length of the lizard at adult size. The height should be about the same as the width—remember that you will usually be using a deep substrate when keeping these lizards. Therefore with a basic calculation we can see that that a 3-inch (7.6 cm) lizard would require a 15-inch (38.1-cm) long and 9-inch (22.9-cm) wide terrarium.

Substrate

Substrates are the materials used on the floor of the enclosure to provide stable footing, waste absorption, and other benefits. Which substrate is best is probably the most controversial subject in uromastyx husbandry. There are many opinions about this subject. It will be helpful to examine each substrate in turn. When using any substrate that allows for burrowing, such as sand or birdseed, the substrate should be at least 4 inches (10.2 cm) deep.

Sand, fine gravel, sod, birdseed, newspaper, alfalfa pellets, and indoor/outdoor carpeting have all been used as substrates within uromastyx enclosures with some degree of success. Experienced keepers and breeders do not use gravel as a substrate for uros. Gravel is implicated in gut impactions, a serious condition in which the particles of gravel block up the digestive tract. Additionally, gravel is hard to clean; moisture from the uro's wastes tends to pool underneath it.

Carpet Substrates

Indoor/outdoor carpeting is another substrate avoid. A uro's claws apparently can easily become entangled within the loops of the carpeting and be wound so tightly that the loops act as a tourniquet. Uros can also wrap a loop around their necks and therefore strangle themselves attempting to escape the binding. I have seen many lizards with missing toes and even heard stories of their dying when being kept on this substrate.

Cage carpet is another substrate that can be used for reptiles; it is similar to indoor/outdoor carpeting but is manufactured specifically for use in herp cages. Because uromastyx are natural burrowers, this is not a good substrate for them. Presumably they can't tear through the carpet by simply clawing at it, and supposedly they can not get bits of it wrapped around the toes as they could with indoor/outdoor carpeting. However, cage carpet still allows moisture from wastes to pool underneath it. According to manufacturers, it is easily cleaned by simply removing the carpet, washing it, and replacing it when dried. Keepers using this substrate should keep an extra piece on hand so that while one is drying, there is still a substrate in the enclosure.

Sod

Sod has been used with some success as a uromastyx substrate, but it seems to be an extremely difficult substrate to work with and use without endangering your lizard. The very first issue that comes to mind is the fact that sod farms use chemical fertilizers to grow their sod. If the uromastyx ingests the grass—likely, since it has a natural diet of grasses—this might lead it to be poisoned. Secondly, the high heats at which uromastyx must be kept are not conducive to the growth of sod. We must also take into account the fact that humidity that would result from the use of sod, because sod requires a certain amount of water. Humidity in a uromastyx enclosure usually is a death sentence. All of these factors add up to sod's not being a good substrate for uros in most cases.

Most keepers and breeders house their uromastyx on a substrate of sand, shown here with Indian uros.

Alfalfa Pellets

A number of keepers use alfalfa pellets successfully. These are beneficial to the uromastyx in that they can be eaten without ill effects. Not to mention that they are also a good source of nutrition for the uro. Alfalfa pellets are also a great absorptive material when it comes to waste elements.

There are a number of drawbacks to an alfalfa pellet substrate. They are unnatural-looking and visually unappealing. They are slightly more difficult to spot-clean when compared to some other substrates. They are somewhat dusty and can become extremely foul-smelling if they get wet and are allowed to mold. Also, if they get moldy it is probably unhealthy for your uro to eat them.

Newspaper

The old faithful of the reptile world is newspaper. It has been used for many years, and

Seed Pests

Birdseed often comes with hitchhikers. These are insects, usually the larvae of moths and beetles. To prevent an outbreak of moths in your home, you should not buy seed that has moths or worms in it or any seed that contains webs. If you do end up with a batch of seed that has bugs, you can kill them by freezing the seed for about 8 hours before use.

there is no evidence it poses any health hazards. The major complaint about newspaper as a substrate is that it is just plain unattractive.

Newspaper does have a big disadvantage when keeping uromastyx. These are burrowing lizards; newspapers will obviously not allow this behavior. I have heard of people keeping their uros on shredded newspaper that the lizards can tunnel into without any obvious ill effects. This is typically reserved for the housing of neonates, because of the danger they will consume other substrates. Newspaper is an extremely absorbent material, as well as being cheap. While you can use newspaper in quarantine setups, I recommend using plain paper towels for this purpose because there is no risk posed by ink.

Birdseed

Uromastyx breeder Jeff Fischer has introduced the use of birdseed to uromastyx keepers, and some keepers who have used it believe it to be a good alternative to the other substrates available. This substrate is used and recommended by some breeders today with a high success rate. It is light in weight and provides some nutritional value should the uro decide to eat it. It isn't the most attractive or naturalistic substrate. If used with neonates it can

Incidential Tasting

A behavior common to many species of lizards (especially desert-dwelling species) is "incidental tasting." This behavior is seen most often when there is a new item added to the enclosure or when the substrate has been changed. Typically what occurs is that after the item is added or the substrate changed the lizard wanders around seemingly trying to identify what has changed. To do this it sticks out its tongue and pulls it back into the mouth in a somewhat snakelike fashion. Although a uro sometimes gets some substrate stuck to the tongue, this has never led to an impaction in my experience.

cause impaction, as would sand and other particulate substrate, but otherwise it is fine.

Sand

Sand—specifically the play sand sold for children's sandboxes—in my opinion is the best substrate for any desert lizard and especially for uromastyx. It is extremely cheap when you buy it in 50-pound (22.7-kg) bags. It is also easy to spot-clean with a screen scoop similar to a cat box scooper but made from wire instead of plastic. Some keepers say that play sand can harbor parasites, but I have personally never had any problems with this occurring. The major drawback to using play sand is its sheer weight. Make no mistake, a uro cage when fully decorated may weigh somewhere around 200 or more pounds (90.7 kg), at least 100 of those pounds (45.4 kg) being just the sand by itself.

Something that should also be mentioned here is that different types of play sand are available. You should always check the size of the grains before purchase to make

North African uromastyx making use of the clothes dryer flex pipe provided to them as artificial burrows.

sure that the grains are fine and not too large. One grain when looking at the sand itself should be smaller than the head of straight pin. This type of sand will not cause impaction.

There are other types of sand available beside play sand, some of which are packed specifically for use in reptile enclosures. These are usually much more expensive than play sands and do not seem to be any safer for your lizard.

Some of these sands are made of some type of calcium and claim to be good for your reptile to eat. This has led to people not giving their reptiles calcium— and this is to be avoided at all times. Just because your reptile is eating the calcium substrate doesn't mean you shouldn't dose the food with calcium. Another concern with this substrate is the possibility that the uro may become overdosed with calcium, which would cause further health issues. A few people have raised the issue of impaction with this type of substrate as well.

Clay-Based Substrates

A new product that may make a suitable substrate for uros is one composed of a clay mixture. The new product holds its structure when you mold it, just as modeling clay would, so you can form caves and burrows for your desert-dwelling reptile. It hardens and compacts when dry while retaining its shape. You can form caves and bolt holes and then add sand or another substrate on top of it. This allows the animal to form its own burrows and also allows you to have burrows far underneath the surface, mimicking the natural habitat of uromastyx and other desert lizards. Covering the clay substrate with sand extends the lifetime of the clay substrate, because you can spot-clean the sand. In most cases it is recommended that you change the entire substrate every four months.

When using above-ground pipes as uro burrows, provide a hide box on at least one end. In this photo the lid of the hide box was removed to show the lizard and substrate.

As with any particulate substrate, people have voiced their concerns about ingestion of the clay mixture, which might lead to impaction issues. Ingestion through incidental tasting as most uromastyx do is not at all harmful. But should your uromastyx break a piece off and ingest it for some reason, there would be a risk of impaction.

Another warning on the packaging tells the keeper not to use undertank heaters in conjunction with the clay substrate. Through a brief correspondence with one manufacturer via e-mail, I have discovered that there is a potential for heat encapsulation because of the thickness of this particular substrate. The substrate will trap the heat, causing it to build up under the tank and in the lowest layers of the substrate. This may cause stress cracks in a glass tank.

Substrates and Gut Impaction

Many reptile hobbyists are concerned about the risk of gut impaction posed by various substrates; there are numerous opinions on the subject but few real facts. Impaction seems to occur because the reptile is being allowed to ingest the substrate. To prevent this particular behavior, offer food within a controlled area such as a food bowl. I have seen uros drop food outside the bowl and then eat it, but this has never caused impaction. If the lizards are ingesting substrate, they may be doing so because of mineral deficiencies in their diets. Anecdotal evidence suggests that adding a mineral supplement to the diet causes the lizard to stop eating substrate.

Furniture

Furnishing the uro enclosure is a relatively easy process, but there are some things to keep in mind and some problems to avoid. One of these problems is trying to decide which décor items to choose. There is a wide range of materials that work well in a uromastyx enclosure.

Prefabricated hide boxes available at pet stores are useful for hatchlings, such as these ornates.

On the Ledge

Rocky outcroppings of some kind are essential when keeping uros. These items allow uros to have perching areas as well as providing some hide crevices, adding to the uro's psychological well being.

Tunnels and Burrows

You should provide all species of uromastyx with some type of burrow or tunnel—or at the minimum a cave structure—that they can go to when attempting to escape either a cage mate or a passerby. These hideaways can be constructed from clay pipes, PVC pipes, or flex pipe (the piping used on the back of clothes dryers to vent out the hot air). I wouldn't recommend the use of the flex pipe, as it has low tensile strength. Should you decide to use these types of tubes I would highly recommend that they be used above the substrate only; if the substrate is on top of these pipes, they could collapse on your lizard. Whichever pipe type you choose should be large enough for the uro to move through comfortably. This means the tube will need to be about 3 inches (7-8 cm) wider than the widest part of the uro who will use it.

Keepers with large enclosures sometimes use patio blocks as both hiding areas and basking sites.

They should be placed at a 45° angle, with the top opening of the pipe being roughly on the level of the top of the substrate, allowing the uro to enter. I have seen it recommended that the pipe itself should have a 45° or 90° bend at the end beneath the substrate as well. It has always been a concern of mine that when using bends at the ends of the pipes the lizard may become stuck. I have never read about or heard of this being reported, but it has always been a concern for me and I have therefore never kept my animals in such a way.

Once the burrow is in place, the uro will travel down this artificial burrow and build itself a resting chamber at the end. Some keepers use a variation on burrow construction: the pipes are left above the surface of the substrate and a hide box is attached to one end.

When using pipes for a uromastyx enclosure, you should place a hide box on each end of the pipe. This will give the lizard a greater feeling of security. It will also allow the uro to come out into the top hide without having to fully expose itself. The hide itself has two exits, one leading into the burrow and one leading out into the enclosure.

Within my personal collections I have kept uros without burrows and have had success doing so. Be that as it may, a colleague and I once built burrows for his uromastyx collection, which were kept in large livestock troughs. We took molded plastic snake hides made to appear like rock and placed baked clay pipes at their entrance. These were put in the bottoms of the troughs and then covered with play sand. The pipes angled up so one end stuck out of the surfaces. The uros used them immediately, and we never had any type of accident where anything collapsed in upon them.

Caves

You can use caves in your uromastyx enclosure, either instead of or in addition to tunnels and burrows. You will have to construct these caves yourself, but this is not too difficult. In some areas you can even go out and find your own rocks. When I did this, a friend and I drove out to the desert and picked up approximately 50 pounds (22.7 kg) of rock. Picking up rocks in the wild should be done carefully, causing minimal disturbance to natural habitat. Rocks that slide off outcroppings or that were unearthed during a building project are good choices.

If you do not live near a desert you may be able to pick up flagstone or some other type of stone at a local home center or hardware store where pathway stones are sold. Stones in these places may be expensive. However, you should try to talk to the manager or owner to see if they have some scrap material that they would be willing to let go for a much cheaper price.

Once you have your rocks, use silicone aquarium sealant (to ensure the safety of your pet, don't use any other type of adhesive, which may give off toxic fumes) to glue them together to create a series of caves big enough for your uros to hide in. In my enclosure the cave structure covered one side and approximately half of the back of a 125-gallon (473.2-liter) enclosure. The lizards seemed very happy, which they exhibited through their behaviors; they all had caves and basking areas of their own. In addition, shedding was facilitated by use of the rough rocks that were glued into the cave system.

You must be absolutely sure that the rocks are either securely buried or otherwise fixed to the terrarium floor. It is imperative that they be set up in such a way that a rambunctious uromastyx will not be able to knock them over.

Cleaning this particular type of set-up is easier if the rock structure can be taken apart, for example if you were to silicone sections together while others were fixed to the enclosure itself. Another option would be to purchase or find a large piece of slate and silicone the smaller rocks to it accordingly. You may decide to use several smaller

Uromastyx will appreciate having access to rocky crevices and ledges within their enclosures.

Check Before Your Collect

If you live close enough to a desert to collect rocks there, you should first call the park ranger or other such authority in the area that you will be collecting in. You may discover that there is no collecting allowed due to local, state, or federal regulations. It is best to actually call rather than getting the information off a website. The reason for this is that laws are constantly changing and governments and other agencies can be slow in updating their respective websites. You don't want to be in the middle of the desert collecting rocks and wind up collecting a hefty fine instead.

rock piles just placed close together. With this technique, you can silicone smaller rocks to appropriately sized pieces of slate to prevent toppling. You can attach (with bolts or silicone) flat pieces of slate to the bottom of the enclosure. Therefore stacking is easier because you have a stable section attached to the base of the enclosure. The general idea is that any caves or other features you construct must be stable enough to withstand the actions of a rambunctious uro.

It's a good idea to have a couple of pieces of slate or flat stone that could be attached by silicone on top of the caves. Basically you will silicone the caves to the flat base and then on top of the cave you will silicone another piece of slate or flat rock. This will allow the uro to bask happily on a flat surface as well as providing a hide beneath, where it can retreat for cover.

For most uromastyx keepers who will have single animals or pairs, the typical molded plastic hiding places available in pet stores will be more than sufficient. Many of these are difficult to tell from actual rocks without actually handling them.

Recommended Precaution

Any décor, whether collected or purchased, should be thoroughly disinfected. A safe and inexpensive disinfectant is solution of 10 percent bleach and water. Rinse the items thoroughly so that you can smell no more bleach on them. If the décor is collected (rocks, branches, etc.), I always bake it in the oven at 400°F (204.4°C) for 15 minutes. This should ensure that any critters or pathogens will be dead. I have used this method for years and never had any reptile in my care become sick from items added to their enclosure.

Backgrounds and Ledges

A background adds some depth to the appearance of the enclosure. If your enclosure is a glass aquarium, the background will also hide unsightly wires from the lights.

Polystyrene backgrounds that look like natural surroundings are available. There are many shapes and colors to choose from. There is also at least one brand of background that has ledges for herps to perch on. Some brands are attached to the back of the terrarium with Velcro, but it is best to use silicone aquarium sealant to provide a permanent fit and to ensure that the weight of an adult uromastyx doesn't cause the Velcro to fail.

There are also molded plastic ledges that give the appearance of rock that you can silicone together and have the look of natural rock piles. With the molded plastic style, I would refrain from trying to cut these and shape them to fit. The reason for this is they may crack under the pressure of the cutting. Use aquarium silicone on the plastic molded parts to attach them to a large piece of slate as a base so your construction will not be able to topple over onto the lizard. Be aware that some plastic pieces have sharp edges on which the uro might be able to cut itself. Sandpaper or a file can be used to smooth the edges of these pieces without issue.

Climbing Branches

If you want to keep *U. benti*, I would highly suggest housing it or them with some type of climbing branch or limb, as this species is known to climb in the wild. With all species, I usually keep some type of limb or grapevine just to add to the appearance of the overall setup.

Lighting

One of the most important aspects when it comes to the husbandry of uromastyx species is that of lighting. We must understand that these desert lizards are sun-loving to the extreme; the radiation from the sun itself actually helps with the digestion and growth of these animals. Knowing this, keepers must provide them with the equivalent of natural sunlight. Although housing uromastyx outside with daily access to sunlight is possible, it is improbable that the average keeper has enough room, time, or resources to keep uros in the outdoors with sufficient heat to keep them healthy throughout the entire year. Therefore uros usually are housed indoors and provided an alternative to the natural sunlight that they would obtain by basking normally in the wild.

Reptile hobbyists provide their pets with the necessary types of light through various types of bulbs. You can purchase these bulbs from most pet shops. Some types may also be available at hardware stores and plant nurseries. There are also numerous online vendors selling reptile lighting.

Types of Light

Reptile keepers are often encouraged to provide a "full-spectrum" bulb when keeping any type of diurnal lizard, including uromastyx. However, when it comes to "full-spectrum" lighting, many people misunderstand what this term actually means. Today many of the various reptile bulbs—both incandescent and fluorescent—claim to be "full-spectrum," but this claim may mean different things. Most of the bulbs differ in the wavelengths of ultraviolet light (UV) they produce. Ultraviolet radiation is divided into three categories. These three categories are UVA, which is the longest of the wavelengths, UVB is the mid wavelength, and lastly UVC is the short wavelength of the ultraviolet wavelengths. As of this

Rock Stores

Masonry centers carry a large selection of rocks, bricks, and other materials that can possibly be used for building perches, basking areas, and hides. Your local home improvement store may have items as well.

writing, there has been no demonstrable proof that "true" full-spectrum lighting providing UVA, UVB, and UVC has any advantageous or disadvantageous effects on the health of captive reptiles. However, there is proof positive that some reptiles and especially diurnal vegetarian lizards do require at a minimum a source of UVB lighting in order to process and metabolize calcium. There is some evidence also that UVA is important for breeding.

The ultraviolet B waves trigger the synthesis of vitamin D3 within the skin of most vertebrates, including both humans and uromastyx. In nature, it is believed that diurnal lizards naturally regulate their absorption of vitamins and minerals through their basking behaviors. A study done by J. R. Jones in 1996 showed that panther chameleons (*Chamaeleo pardalis*) would move to places where they could increase their exposure to UV light if given such an opportunity. I have observed this in my own collection. My lizards will bask under the UV-providing bulbs even when other basking and perching sites are available. They move back and forth between basking lights and the UV-generating lights.

Suffice it to say that enough research has been done and it has been proven time and again that diurnal herbivorous lizards require an uncertain amount of UVB lighting. I say an uncertain amount because I have yet to find anyone or any study that can show beyond a reasonable doubt an exact measure of how much UVB is required and used by our reptilian companions.

UVA lighting typically is ignored by most who keep uromastyx or any other diurnal lizard as pets. At first glance this may not seem as a detrimental factor to be concerned with when keeping diurnal lizards. It has been shown, however, by William H. Gehrmann, PhD in a study published by the Society for the Study of Amphibians and Reptiles that UVA could influence reproductive and signaling behaviors in some lizards. Prolific reptile care author Melissa Kaplan states that UVA exposure from mercury vapor

Unless you can keep your uro outdoors, you will have to provide it with full-spectrum lighting. A basking ocellated uromastyx is shown here.

lamps played a major role in the elicitation of normal aggressive behavior in desert iguanas (*Dipsosaurus dorsalis*), collared lizards (*Crotophytus collaris*), and rainbow lizards (*Agama agama*).

The UVA in natural sunlight seems to elicit feeding responses, as it allows the diurnal lizards to identify by the colors of what plants they would feed on in the wild. It is also believed that UVA allows diurnal lizards to obtain certain visual cues needed for breeding.

Types of Bulbs

Fluorescent Bulbs One of the most widely used bulbs in the reptile hobby is fluorescent tubes. There are a number of different brands available, and a number of different bulbs within those brands. Each bulb provides a slightly different spectrum of light. When keeping uromastyx, it is critical that the keeper look for the UVB content, as well as making sure the bulb provides UVA. Recently a bulb containing 10 percent UVB has come on the market. This particular fluorescent bulb provides an intensity currently unrivaled in the reptile industry, according to the independent studies I have read. While these bulbs are commonly used and provide good illumination and ultraviolet output, they do have some drawbacks. The first drawback is that they tend to be expensive. Related to this, they also need to be replaced every 6 to 12 months. Although the bulbs still produce visible light after this time, they lose the capability of producing ultraviolet light.

Uromastyx will show their best colors only when kept under the proper lighting. This is an orange phase Saharan uromastyx.

Mercury Vapor Lamps There is another light source available one that can lead you to believe that you are getting a two-for-one deal (heat and UV in one package). These are known as mercury vapor lamps; they may not be the best bulbs to use with uromastyx, however. They are very expensive and don't necessarily produce as much UV as the packages may state. These bulbs do produce a lot of heat, making them a reasonable choice for heating the terrarium.

One reason they do not produce the promised amounts of UV is that they may shut off on their own at any moment. This is caused by a device known as the ballast. This device shuts the bulb off if it becomes too hot, and these bulbs typically get *very* hot. The ballast on these bulbs allows them to recognize when they get to a certain temperatures that may damage them or cause an early burnout; they automatically shut off to prevent the light from overheating. Therefore during their off periods they are not providing any UV light at all. This in turn may lead to the uro's suffering from lack of vitamin D3.

To counteract this you must use a thermostat, which will control the temperature of the lamp so as not to let it overheat. Some authors/keepers claim that this type of light puts out too much UV, which requires you to shut them off when working near them. I personally have yet to read any such evidence that this type of lighting might be harmful to either the reptile or the human keeper. In fact I have had correspondence with keepers who have used them for years and bred many lizards under such conditions with no ill effects whatsoever.

Not Always Double the Fun

If you are planning to house more than one uromastyx in a single enclosure you must absolutely make sure that you provide multiple basking and hide areas. The reason for this is that uros may and typically will establish a pecking order that could lead to one of them becoming malnourished and generally stressed by the bullying. By providing these multiple basking and hide areas the less dominant individuals are given the opportunity to regulate their temperature and feel comfortable. I would also highly recommend multiple feeding bowls or sites in order to curb any food-related aggression.

Tungsten Filament Lamps Tungsten filament lamps are also sold in reptile stores, and some claim that they are a good source of UVB. Tungsten lamps are incapable of providing UVB and should only be used to provide heat or visibility. Some may provide some UVA, but the levels are debatable.

Metal Halide Bulbs Yet another lighting source available but not recommended is the metal halide bulb. These lights seem to produce much too much UVA, which may cause cancers in reptiles. A few independent studies conducted by reptile owners themselves have suggested this to be true. They produce less UVB light than the aforementioned fluorescent lights. They do provide a lot of heat, visible light, UVA, and some UVB.

Day/Night Cycle

Another factor that must be mentioned here is the length of time that the uromastyx should be exposed to the UVA and UVB lighting. My recommendation is to use normal daylight cycles that occur naturally. In other words, unless you live somewhere where there is not a "normal" twelve-hour cycle of night and day, then provide the UVA and UVB in amounts equal to the day length in you location.

Being we all live extremely busy lives, it is easy to forget to turn the lights on and off. To prevent this, buy a timer from a home improvement store and you totally eliminate the possibility of forgetting to turn the lights on. Set the timer to turn the lights on around 6 a.m. and shut off around 6 p.m. I have used this regimen for years without ill effects in my uros. I also shut off the heat about 30 to 45 minutes before the UV goes out. This is something that I have recently begun doing in order to simulate the evening cooling period that the lizards would experience in wild.

Replacing Bulbs

Something else a keeper must always remember and should be very careful of is replacement of the UV bulbs. The bulbs must be replaced according to the manufacturers' instructions—typically this will be every 6 to 12 months. I replace mine religiously every 6 months, regardless of what the manufacturer suggests. The reason for this is that they simply lose the intensity of their UV output over time.

Bulb Replacement

Ultraviolet bulbs should be replaced roughly every six months. Although many manufacturers state that their bulbs produce UVB for longer than this, most studies show this is usually not the case. To remember when to replace your bulbs, write the date you install the bulb on the bulb itself and also put the date on a calendar six months in advance.

Like most animals, uromastyx need a regular day/night cycle for optimum health.

Bulb Placement

For your uro to reap the benefits of UV lighting, it must be able to bask within about 12 inches (30.5 cm) of the bulb. Bulbs should provide the same amount of radiance across the entire enclosure. The reasoning behind this is that most reptiles gravitate towards the heat only when necessary for basking. At those times they would not be exposed to the UV lights. By running the UV lights across the entire enclosure, your uros get the needed exposure. This is easily done with fluorescent bulbs, but in my experience it is much harder to do with the incandescent styles, because you would need several incandescent bulbs placed throughout the enclosure to ensure full coverage.

Personal Choice

In the end, it comes down to personal opinions. Given the options, I at one time would have said that a uromastyx keeper should use a fluorescent light for UV and a separate incandescent light to provide heat. Today, after reading the available independent research, I

Use a Probe

Thermometers with an external probe are more accurate than any of the types that stick on the enclosure wall. This is because you can use the probe to measure the exact temperature at the basking site, which might be significantly different from the temperature on the glass.

have begun changing all of my terrariums to the use of incandescent mercury bulbs with thermostats in order to better replicate the natural environments of my lizards.

Heating

To most people who have never kept uromastyx the recommended keeping temperatures may seem extreme. However, remember that these particular saurians come from some of the hottest places on earth. In some of their habitats, the temperature may reach over 122°F (50°C). Uromastyx need a basking spot that reaches 115°F (46.1°C), but the rest of the enclosure should be kept at 85°F (29.4°C) during the day. At night the temperatures can drop down to around 75°F (23.9°C). Once again, there are choices to be made when it comes to heating. Which method or combination of methods you use depends on your personal preference and individual keeping situation.

Heat Lamps

There are several kinds of heat lamps available for use in reptile enclosures. Some also produce UV light; these were discussed in the lighting section. Here the discussion is solely about using lamps for heating.

Incandescent bulbs produce high amounts of both heat and light. They are excellent for raising the ambient

Heat lamps are the most common method for heating uros. They provide both warmth and illumination.

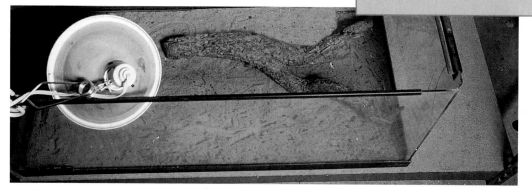

temperature in the enclosure and providing a hot basking spot. You can control the temperature these lamps produce by changing the wattage of the bulbs or by suspending the lamp higher or lower above the enclosure as needed.

Red incandescent bulbs sold by most reptile stores are another common way to heat uromastyx. They are relatively inexpensive and provide needed heat. As with other incandescents, you carefully must match the size of the bulb to the enclosure you're trying to heat. They also provide some viewing of your lizards at night if you should so desire. By using a lower-wattage bulb than you use for daytime heating, you can provide a nighttime temperature drop that mimics the conditions uros would experience in nature.

Metal halide bulbs and mercury vapor bulbs produce high levels of heat while also generating UV light. The pros and cons of these bulbs are discussed in the lighting section.

Ceramic Heating Elements

One useful heating device for uromastyx enclosures is a ceramic heating element (also called ceramic heat emitter). These are interesting little mechanisms that provide heat without light, making them excellent for nighttime heating. They are durable and long-lasting, producing high levels of heat for the wattage.

Lighting Fixtures

Any incandescent lighting or ceramic heating element should be put into a reflecting dome fixture; this can be placed in suspension over the basking area or inside the cage itself. If you put the fixture inside the cage, it is critical that the uromastyx cannot reach it. I have

Seeing Red

Conventional wisdom within the herp hobby states that reptiles can't see the red wavelengths of light. This belief is encouraged by the manufacturers' stating on the packaging of red bulbs that the red light will be less disturbing to the day-night cycle of the herp. The truth of the matter is that some reptiles can actually see the red much better than we can. So leaving red bulbs on at night can interrupt the circadian rhythms of sleep and rest. In a manner of speaking using this type of bulb would be akin to keeping your reptile in permanent sunset. It is still not certain whether these bulbs disturb herps or not, but it is a possibility.

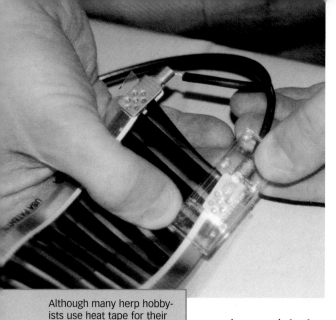

Although many herp hobbyists use heat tape for their animals, it can be difficult to use correctly.

done this by actually recessing the fixture into the cage, leaving the back part of it sticking out of the lid of the enclosure and placing a screen mesh over the opening. However, it is easier and safer to use the fixture outside the cage by either resting it on the screen top or suspending it above the enslcosure.

There are two different types of lighting fixtures. Some have plastic sockets and some have ceramic sockets where the light is to be screwed in. With the high heat put out by a uro's basking lights and heat emitters, plastic sockets may actually melt. It is better to spend a little extra money and get a ceramic socket.

Heat Tapes

Many herp authors and breeders recommend using plumbing-style heat tapes to heat pet herps. Herpetoculturists have used it for years in breeding racks. However, heat tape was not manufactured for heating herps and needs to be installed correctly. There is a significant risk of installing it incorrectly and consequently damaging either the enclosure or the reptile or even worse starting a fire resulting from faulty wiring—a number of herp hobbyists have burned down their houses in just this way. A few companies offer a specific type of heat tape and the proper connections in order to make it work. The drawback to these heat tapes is that they do not get hot enough for uromastyx, so the keeper will need to use them combined with some other heating device.

Undertank Heater

Undertank heaters are sold in pet stores and are manufactured for use with herps in glass enclosures. They adhere below the undersurface of the tank and provide heat to a section of the substrate. Most of them do not heat the tank higher than about 10°F (5.6°C) warmer than the outside temperature; obviously this by itself is not warm enough for uromastyx.

They also do not work well when you're trying to heat a custom-made wooden enclosure or a metal watering trough. They can, however, provide supplemental heat when used in conjunction with ceramic heating element or incandescent heat bulbs.

Heating Mats

Heating mats or pads are also available from some herpetological retailers. These were originally developed for use with farm animals, although there are now some designed for use with herps. They are waterproof and tear resistant. Most manufacturers that sell these types of heating elements also sell some type of thermostat to go with it, which you should always use. There is a possibility that these devices will not raise the ambient temperatures, and therefore the reptile would attempt to continually bask on them and be burned.

Radiant Heat Panels

Radiant heat panels are one more source for heating. They are similar to undertank heaters, but they are safe to put inside the enclosure. You affix them to the back wall or the ceiling of the enclosure. Once inside the enclosure they emit over a large area. Make sure your uro cannot entangle itself on the electrical cord.

Hot Rocks

Hot rocks are made of resin or similar material molded around a heat-producing coil. Never under any circumstances should you use one of these to try to heat your enclosure. There are countless documented cases of lizards attempting to get warm lying on these and becoming horribly burned, sometimes dying from their injuries. This is because if you count on the hot rock to heat the enclosure, the air temperature will be too cool. Your lizard will be forced to lie directly on the stone all the time to stay warm. The end result is a burned belly. Some keepers have success using these devices as supplemental heating units, but this is still risky.

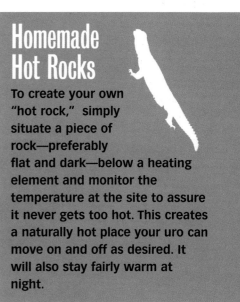

Homemade Hot Rocks

To create your own "hot rock," simply situate a piece of rock—preferably flat and dark—below a heating element and monitor the temperature at the site to assure it never gets too hot. This creates a naturally hot place your uro can move on and off as desired. It will also stay fairly warm at night.

Thermometers

Uromastyx require enclosure temperatures that range from 85°F (29.4°C) to 115 (46.1°C) at the basking site. You cannot safely just guess at or estimate these temperatures; buy a decent thermometer and be sure. One of the best types of thermometers is a digital one with an external probe. These are highly accurate, and most can record the lowest and highest temperatures in a 24-hour period. Infrared temperature guns are another very accurate temperature gauge. Thermometers that stick on the glass are useful only to a point. They are good for measuring the ambient temperature but are not good for measuring the basking-site temperature. The sticker type on the wall near the basking site may read 85°F (29.4°C) while the actual temperature right below the basking light is 105 (40.6°C)—a 20 degree difference! This could lead to overheating or underheating your uro.

It's a good idea to have two thermometers. Place one at the basking area and another at the cool end of the enclosure, as far away from the basking light as possible. This allows you to make absolutely sure that you are providing your lizard with the proper temperature gradient.

Thermostats and Rheostats

These two items play a large role in the proper heating of reptiles, particularly species that need the high temperatures that uromastyx do. It is common to sell these items together and discuss them as though they were the same thing. Nevertheless, thermostats and rheostats are two completely different mechanisms.

When not warm enough, uros will be dull brown or gray in color, as these Mali uromastyx are.

Thermostats Thermostats are used for controlling temperature within an enclosure at any given time. Typically speaking, they are plugged in outside the enclosure, and a probe is usually placed somewhere near the heated side of the enclosure. When the probe detects that a specific temperature has been reached, it opens the circuit and thereby turns the heating element off. Conversely, when the temperature drops below a preset temperature, the thermostat closes and turns the heating element on. The constant on and off action of the element significantly shortens its lifespan.

Placing a flat rock directly beneath the heat lamp creates a nice basking spot for your uro. This hatchling Saharan uro is basking in just such a setup.

Most of the thermostats produced today automatically turn off when they reach 110° F (43.3°C). As stated earlier, uros need a basking area of 115° (46.1°C). Therefore it is difficult to use a thermostat to keep the basking spot in a uromastyx enclosure at the proper temperature.

At least one thermostat is available that keeps the element at a lower-than-maximum operating temperature and doesn't actually turn the bulb on or off but instead increases or decreases the intensity of the output. Another interesting feature on this particular thermostat is that it has a nighttime temperature-drop feature, which is enabled by the use of a simple timer.

Keeping your uro's enclosure clean will go along way toward keeping it healthy. A Yemeni uromastyx is shown.

Rheostats Rheostats are not at all like thermostats, as they only increase or decrease the intensity of a heating element or light. If you have ever used a dimmer switch in your home you are more than familiar with what rheostats can do. These devices must be actively used. In other words, unless you are there to manually effect the turning of the knob they are of no use. This is especially true if you have purchased the correct intensity of heating element for your specific enclosure.

Some companies have a recommendation on the packaging stating something to the effect that the enclosed product is best used when ambient temperatures are stable. These items are reputed to burn up and become stuck in place if left at one setting for a continuous period of time. I therefore recommend against using these types of devices when it comes to heating any reptile enclosure.

Maintenance

Pet lizards are very dependent on their human caretakers. They are different from our

Uromastyx Cleaning and Maintenance Schedule

Daily	Weekly	Monthly
Remove food bowl and scrub	Sift entire enclosure	Change all Substrate
Spot-clean feces and any uneaten food	Scrub and disinfect all hides and decor	Disinfect entire enclosure

mammal companions, who can typically bark or emote in some way that they need something. So when it comes to maintaining your uromastyx, it may be easy to forget to perform certain tasks, as our modern lives of are full of work, family, and other activities we enjoy. Be sure to observe the uro for any signs that it is not in optimal health as well. The observant keeper will notice that the lizard is out of sorts or may be exhibiting behavior that is "unusual."

Reptiles do not have the capability of letting us know what they need—or at least humans have no way of detecting their moods. Therefore we have to be observant, and it is best to set up a regimen of some type or write yourself a note on the calendar. Refer to the accompanying chart for a schedule of tasks a uro keeper must perform.

Each day you will need to remove uneaten food, clean the feeding bowl, and spot-clean any feces or pieces of shed skin you find. Every week you should sift the entire substrate and clean and disinfect all furnishings. Sifting means to take a cat box scooper (there are also products manufactured to sift sand in herp enclosures) and run it through all the substrate to remove any debris. Disassemble all the furnishings and scrub off feces, uneaten food, or other dirt. Then soak them in a 10 percent bleach solution or cook them in the oven at 400°F (204.4°C) for 10 to 15 minutes as explained earlier. Rinse thoroughly and re-place.

Monthly, you will need to replace the entire substrate and wash and disinfect the entire enclosure and its furnishings. Spray down the enclosure with the bleach solution or some type of pet-safe disinfectant. Make sure that after rinsing and airing out the enclosure, no smell of bleach or disinfectant remains when you reassemble it and put your uro back inside.

Chapter 4

Feeding and Nutrition

With all the vegetables that are available for human consumption, it would be easy to become anthropomorphic when feeding our reptiles. Resist this temptation at all costs. Reptiles, and especially uromastyx, must be fed a diet that approximates what they would be eating in nature. It must be a diet that allows their natural processes to pull necessary nutrients out of their food and expel their wastes. While this may seem a bland diet of eating what amounts to salads to every day, it is the closest substitution that we as keepers are able to provide when compared with the lizards' diet in the wild.

Uromastyx in nature are almost totally herbivorous animals and must be fed accordingly when kept as pets.

Some authors suggest that we read the government's recommended diet to learn which greens are safe. This is strange when you consider that the human digestive system is significantly different from that of a uromastyx. There is little reason why we would read the information for human consumption of vegetables and in turn feed a similar diet to our reptiles. These types of tables and recommendations can be used as a starting reference point, but it is important to keep in mind the vast differences between a human's digestive system and a uromastyx's.

Diet in Nature

First we'll look at the diet of species in the wild. *U. a. microlepis* has been observed eating mostly grasses such as *Stipagrostis plumosa* and *Pennisetum divisium capitata* (see Cunningham, P. in the References). These grasses are not readily available in the United States, but uro keepers can find some similar species of plants that can be grown here. Other uro species have been observed eating various species of *Acacia*, *Artemesia*, and *Plantago*. More information on what uros eat in nature is found in Chapter 1.

A uromastyx's digestive system is similar to a horse's or a rabbit's and evolved to digest a diet based on grasses, seeds, leaves, and other plant substances. The specific method of digestion is a process called hindgut fermentation. In this type of digestion, most of the actual breakdown and absorption of nutrients takes place in the large intestine, and a variety of bacteria (also possibly protozoans, fungi, and other microorganisms) participate in the chemical processing of food. Hindgut fermentation is fairly inefficient, and most animals that have this type of digestion evolved to eat large quantities of food that have low nutrient contents, such as grasses.

Although in the wild and in captivity the uros are not really strictly herbivores, keepers should treat them as such. They have been observed in the wild to consume insects occasionally; however, this behavior appears to be purely opportunistic. In other words, if they come across a bug of suitable proportions they'll eat it. Their main food sources are the plants native to their homelands; the uromastyx digestive system is not designed to process any more than just traces of animal matter.

Diet for Pet Uromastyx

The following will be an outline of items including what should and should not be fed to your uromastyx. For a large part, their diets are extremely similar to their distant cousin the green iguana (*Iguana iguana*). Their primary diet should be mainly composed of green leafy vegetables and blooms from various plants. The blooms can be either grown or purchased in some grocery stores. Do not use flowers from florists' shops, because they

Grow Your Own

At least one uromastyx breeder in the US has grown species of *Plantago* and *Zygophyllum* as weeds in his backyard with some success (Douglas Dix, pers. comm.). The keeper who wants to can most likely find seeds for sale via the Internet, or even possibly at an exotic plant society show. Many plants that uromastyx eat are not difficult to grow. If your space is limited, many herbs and flowers will do well when planted in pots sitting on a sunny windowsill. Some options include mints, marigolds, nasturtiums, basil, parsley, and cilantro. If you have a yard, your possibilities for growing uro food are almost limitless.

Many common weeds make good uro food. In this photo the yellow-green stalks are plantains and the white flowers are clovers—uromastyx will enjoy both.

often are treated with preservatives that could harm your lizard. According to some keepers and breeders, you can feed uromastyx insects, such as crickets or mealworms, occasionally.

Feed your uromastyx daily. Offer enough food so that a very small amount is left over at the end of the day. Remove uneaten items before the lights are turned off for the night. Monitor your lizard's weight to be sure you are not feeding too much or too little.

Greens and Other Vegetables

It is easy to supply uros with suitable fare—keepers have to look no further than the local grocery store. You can feed almost any of the dark leafy green vegetable to your saurian companions without fear. Good sources of vitamins and minerals include endive, bok choy, romaine, butter lettuce, watercress, parsley, red leaf lettuce, collard greens, turnip greens, mustard greens, kale, and dandelions (leaves and flowers). Commercially prepared "spring mix" bagged salads make an excellent varied meal for uromastyx. Some plants that you might find growing in your yard can make good uromastyx food as well, provided you do not treat your yard with any chemicals. These include clovers, plantains, grasses, and wild chicory.

However, there are some greens that many keepers advise you to avoid feeding to herps. These include spinach, pigweed, beets, and chard. These plants are members of the goosefoot family, Amaranthaceae. It is known that these plants will block the absorption of calcium in the digestive tracts in mammals. Reptile veterinarians also see many iguanas that are fed a diet high in spinach that are suffering from calcium deficiencies. Although there is no documentation that these plants cause problems for uromastyx, it is better to be safe than sorry. Feed plants of this family in small amounts only. Another green vegetable to be avoided simply because it is mostly water and has almost no nutritional value is iceberg lettuce.

You can grate squash and carrots as a topping for your uro's salad. Cactus (*Optunia* spp.) is used in Mexican food and is excellent for uros and other herbivorous reptiles. Most other

Wash Your Veggies

Unless you purchase your uromastyx's vegetables from a true organic store, you will need to thoroughly wash them in order to rid them of any pesticides and insecticides they may have been sprayed with. It is probably a good idea to wash organic vegetables as well, since they can become contaminated with soil, animal wastes, and organic fertilizers during growth and transport.

fresh vegetables are good to use for variety in a uromastyx's diet. In a pinch, you can use frozen mixed vegetables once in a while. Make sure that they are warmed to room temperature before feeding. While I personally do not offer my

Chopped leafy greens form the base of a healthy uromastyx diet.

Flowers for Supper

Uromastyx seem to really enjoy eating flowers, buds, and blooms. There are many edible flowers that you can offer. You can grow the flowers yourself, and some grocery stores stock edible flowers. Do not use flowers from a florist shop, because they usually have been treated with preservatives. Below is a list of some edible flowers your uro might enjoy

- Clover
- Dandelion
- Honeysuckle
- Lavender
- Marigold
- Nasturtium
- Pansy
- Rose
- Violet

uromastyx fruit, in small amounts it will not cause any harm and adds variety to the diet. It is probably best to avoid citrus and other high-moisture fruits, but apples, pears, figs, and berries should be fine to feed.

Dried Beans

Aside from fresh vegetables, feed your uro a dried bean mix such as a seven-bean dry soup. This provides protein. If you are feeding hatchlings or juvenile uros, grind the beans up in a coffee grinder so they will be small enough for the young lizards to eat. The beans can be sprinkled over the salad of greens you offer daily. Uros should have a supply of dry beans offered daily along with the freshly chopped or grated mixture of greens. Some keepers and breeders also offer small birdseed to their uros for protein. Uromastyx eat grass seeds in nature, so birdseed is similar to components of their natural diet.

Insects

For years there has been debate about whether uromastyx should be fed insects or not. Some authorities say that offering a few occasional insects does no harm and that chasing the insects gives the lizard some necessary exercise. Others are of the opinion that there is absolutely no reason to offer any insects to the uros at all. Which side of the debate should a uro keeper believe?

A study done by Peter Cunningham on U. a. microlepis has shown that less than 1 percent of the entire diet consisted of insect matter. He determined this by studying the fecal matter of wild stock. It is well known that captive uros fed a diet high in insect matter suffer from kidney damage and eventually failure. I recommend feeding insects to uros no more than

once a month. You can offer crickets, mealworms, silk worms, or any of the other insects available as herp food in the pet trade. It can be said that without a doubt uromastyx enjoy their insect fare with complete gusto. While it might be amusing to their human caretaker to watch this, feed insects sparingly.

Wild Insects

Never feed wild-caught insects to your uro. You can't tell whether they have been contaminated with some type of insecticide or pesticide that could potentially harm the uro. There is also a risk that wild-caught insects carry parasites. Always avoid feeding your uromastyx ants, scorpions, bees, wasps, brightly colored insects, spiky or fuzzy caterpillars, and fireflies; these invertebrates are toxic or otherwise dangerous.

Other Items

Frozen vegetable medleys can also be offered as a topping to the fresh greens salad. I have read that the frozen vegetables actually have less nutritional value than fresh vegetables. Frozen vegetables are a good item to keep on hand for days when you have no time to prepare food or when you mistakenly run out of fresh foods.

I have never offered any of the citrus fruits to any of my uros, nor have I heard of other keepers offering citrus. I am concerned with the acidity of such fruits wreaking havoc on the digestive tract.

H_2O: Yes or No?

Currently within the hobby there is a controversy as to whether or not you should keep a water bowl within a uromastyx terrarium. The general point of contention is how damaging the humidity caused by a water bowl is for these lizards. I have personally never used a water source within any of my uromastyx enclosures. In researching this question, I have found no concrete evidence that having water inside the enclosure is beneficial, but it can be harmful. Uromastyx in the wild have never been observed to actually "search" for water. Almost all of the breeders I have spoken with or had any correspondence with agree. Water has no place in the uromastyx environment. However, there are keepers who regularly keep their uromastyx with water and report that they drink and have no issues. Some keepers report that certain species of uromastyx such as *U. geryi*, *U. benti*, and *U. d. maliensis* will readily drink from standing water placed in the enclosure. Still others recommend a short soak on a weekly basis.

I recommend personally against keeping standing water in the enclosure with uromastyx. It has been my personal experience that no uromastyx actually requires a water bowl or other standing water to drink. Because of these lizards' adaptations to their desert environment, they are

Juvenile *U. benti* picking seeds off the ground. Seeds and legumes are an important part of a balanced uromastyx diet.

able to obtain all needed water from their food. Having a water bowl in the enclosure can increase the humidity to levels that are unhealthy for uros.

Vitamin and Mineral Supplements

While vitamins and minerals should be offered to your uromastyx, this should be done in moderation. It has been shown by several authorities that overdosing with certain vitamins will definitely cause problems for uromastyx as well as other species of herbivorous lizards. There are numerous ideas and opinions when it comes to offering mineral and vitamin supplements to uromastyx; there is no one plan that all the authorities agree on.

I recommend adding a powdered calcium supplement to the food every day. This can be lightly dusted over the top of the vegetables. A light dusting means sprinkling the powder supplement just enough for there to be whitish color on the greens. You should not pile the powder on, as this could very easily lead to over-supplementation. Every third day I add a vitamin supplement to the vegetable salad. This in my experience will ensure that the uromastyx will get neither a vitamin nor calcium overdose. Following this regimen, my uros have never had a nutritional problem.

It is important to feed uromastyx birdseed that is not too big for them to eat. Seeds labeled for parakeets and budgies should be the right size.

Vitamins Deficiencies and Overdosing

Given improperly, supplements can cause overdoses of certain vitamins, most often vitamins A and D. But not giving any supplements can lead to deficiencies also, even when the keeper provides a varied diet.

It is highly unlikely that a uromastyx will have a vitamin A deficiency. Leafy green vegetables are high in beta carotene, the natural precursor to vitamin A. It is possible to overdose with this vitamin if you are using a vitamin supplement that is high in vitamin A or are providing too many supplemental vitamins. Using a vitamin supplement that contains beta carotene instead of actual vitamin A should prevent this problem, because excess beta carotene is not converted to vitamin A and is excreted harmlessly.

Vitamin B1 (thiamine) deficiency can be caused by feeding too many frozen vegetables, ferns, and ornamental houseplants. The freezing of vegetables breaks down B vitamins and increases thiaminase, which actually breaks down the uro's stored supply of thiamin.

Deficiencies of vitamins C, E, and K are not common problems in uromastyx unless the keeper is providing a grossly incorrect diet and/or environment.

Calcium, Vitamin D3, and UVB

You may wonder why giving calcium at every feeding is recommended. While pet uromastyx get some calcium from their normal diet, it does not seem to be enough. Additionally, they do not ingest vitamin D3, which is essential for absorbing calcium from the digestive tract. Plants contain vitamin D2, not vitamin D3. Vitamin D2 is less efficient in its role than is D3. So, without supplements, it is likely that a uromastyx is not getting enough calcium. You can dust your uromastyx's food with all the calcium that you want, but it will simply pass out in the animal's urine if it is not exposed to UVB. UVB causes the skin to produce vitamin D3 and therefore absorb calcium from the gut. Some vitamin manufacturers claim that their particular product has vitamin D3 within it. While this is probably true, it is doubtful it is

Pelleted tortoise and iguana foods make a fine emergency food for uromastyx, but they should not be the staple diet.

enough for the needs of diurnal lizards. There is even some debate as to whether some species can absorb vitamin D3 from the diet at all. This is shown to be true by the numerous animals treated for metabolic bone disease by veterinarians where the owners are taught a very hard lesson on vitamin and UVB absorption.

Over-supplementation of vitamin D3 can lead to calcium deposits appearing under the skin as lumps on the muscles and bones, as well as to mineralization of the internal organs in advanced cases. These abnormalities are treatable when caught early, but it has been reported that these deposits can also show up within the heart, which would obviously kill the lizard eventually. Normal exposure to UVB radiation without secondary supplementation of vitamin D3 is the best way to avoid over-supplementation of this vitamin.

Body Spray

One type of vitamin is manufactured to be sprayed on the skin. These products are useless for uromastyx and probably most other lizards. These body vitamin sprays have no way of penetrating the uro's tough outer skin and so at best do the lizards no good. Also, there is the danger that these sprays can raise the humidity in the terrarium, which may cause a respiratory infection.

Spray vs. Powders

There are many products to choose from when looking into the purchase of calcium and vitamin supplements. Two major types of supplements are sprays and powders. Some would argue that sprays are better than powders because they are easier to apply, there is no worrying about dosage issues, they are less messy, etc. Powders, on the other hand, are cheaper when measured out as well as providing a better control over the dosage. There are many theories on which form works best, but when it comes down to it this is a matter of personal choice.

Some authors report that the dosage of the spray supplements is hard to control. The powder can be measured with typical kitchen devices such as teaspoons, tablespoons, etc. Most keepers don't actually measure out the powdered supplements. Some of the products actually don't give any directions whatsoever. Others say things such as "sprinkle lightly." This can be achieved by lightly tapping the side of the bottle while it is slightly tilted over the food. You should have a larger amount of green showing through the dusted vegetables and not a white mountain.

Chapter 5

Breeding

Breeding of any reptile should be primarily taken on because you have an undying passion for the reptile itself. As any reputable breeder can tell you, reptile breeding is expensive and time-consuming. While the rewards can be great, it is typically years before you will see any offspring, and you may never turn a profit.

The Sure Bet

I have always taken my reptiles to a qualified reptile veterinarian in order to have them sexed. While this is more expensive than traditional means, it is almost 100 percent reliable. You should definitely consult a veterinarian to determine the sex of your animals if you are trying to breed a species that is not sexually dimorphic.

With uromastyx it is critical that the potential breeder is attempting the project simply because he or she loves these animals. This is because they are notoriously difficult to breed in captivity, not to mention that the ones that are bred most easily are typically the less attractive species. Knowledgeable herpetoculturists who have bred other species may want to try their hand at breeding these lizards but should remember there are few people who have done so successfully. Those who have done it typically have ten or more years of experience breeding other types of reptiles.

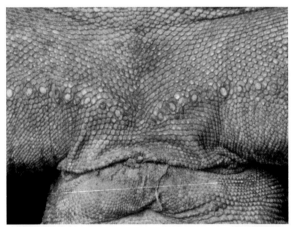

Boys and Girls

While there are some uromastyx species that are sexually dimorphic, there also are those species that are not so easily told apart. Sexually

In some species of uromastyx, mature males develop enlarged pores on the undersurface of the thighs. The pores on this ornate uro (bottom) are excreting a waxy substance believed to be a territorial marker. The pores on the male Egyptian uro (top) are comparatively smaller.

dimorphic means that the males and females have distinctive and distinguishing physical characteristics—in many sexually dimorphic animals, including uros, the males are more colorful than the females. If you are working with a species that is not sexually dimorphic, it is best to have the breeder or a veterinarian determine the sex for you.

With uromastyx species that are sexually dimorphic, a cursory look at the lizard will typically tell you whether it is a male or female. This is especially true when you have two known breeders to compare your choice against. Another way to tell on some but not all species is to look for femoral pores. These pores form a row of pits or openings that run the length of the underside of the thigh. If you see these, the lizard in hand will typically be a male. A uromastyx usually must be at least a year old before the pores become visible. The base of the tail will also be wider in most males than in females, although this may be hard to see unless you

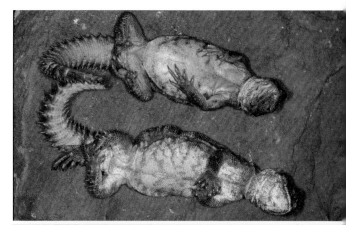

The adults of some species are sexable by color. In the Saharan uromastyx (top), the male is usually much brighter than the female. In the Mali, males (center) are yellow with black head and limbs while the females (bottom) are mottled yellowish brown.

When bringing the
sexes together for
mating, it is best
to introduce the
male to the female's enclosure.
This puts the male in a new
territory, so he will be less likely
to show territorial aggression to
the female. In his own enclosure,
there's a chance the male will
treat the female as an intruder.

have several individuals for comparison. Male uros often exhibit wider heads and a more robust body overall than females.

Another method that has been reported to work well is one that is well proven with bearded dragons (*Pogona vitticeps*). In this method, hold the uro in the flat of the palm with its tail tip pointed down your arm. With your free hand, gently lift the tail and arc it over the Uro's back while watching the cloacal area. If the uro you're holding is a male, you will see a slight dimple appear on the tail just before the cloacal opening. Often the uro will be none too happy about your handling, so perform it over some soft surface. That way if the lizard manages to struggle out of your grip it will not be injured by the fall.

The surest method is to have a reptile veterinarian sex your uromastyx with an x-ray examination. Otherwise, most breeders will be happy to sex your animal before purchase.

Any of the previously mentioned sexing methods will not give reliable results when dealing with babies. Uromastyx cannot be sexed with complete certainty until they are at least six months of age. Even then you must consult an experienced breeder or veterinarian if you want to be as certain as possible.

More Than a Pair

For the best chance at successful breeding, you should have more females than males—one male and two females at a minimum. This is because uros are very aggressive when breeding, and if they are kept in pairs the male may severely injure the lone female in his determination to breed. With two or more females, the male will have the opportunity to achieve breeding without having to get too aggressive towards a single female. In short, his attention will be spread out over multiple females.

Something else that needs mentioning here is that most uromastyx breeders—myself included—have better breeding success when the males and females are housed separately prior to breeding. The sexes are put together only for copulation and then are separated.

Preconditioning

Once you have a mature breeding group, it may seem that you should be able to put them into an enclosure together, put on some groove music, turn the lights down low, and let nature take its course. But it is not that easy. Often you need to put your uros through a process called preconditioning. However, this is not absolutely necessary; some breeders have had success with preconditioning by various methods and some have success with no preconditioning. It is known that breeding without going through preconditioning leads to smaller clutch sizes, health issues for the females, and even sometimes death of the females.

Preconditioning is essentially providing the very best habitat, food, and care, which any keeper should be doing as standard practice. The only difference when pre-conditioning is that the females are typically given a higher dosage of calcium. For example, if you were giving the females calcium once every other day, change that to every day; if you are giving calcium every day, increase the dosage slightly. Vitamin supplements can be provided as usual with no change. The reason we provide extra calcium to the female is to accommodate her with reserve calcium, which will be used to form the eggs.

It is usually best to house male and female uromastyx separately outside of breeding attempts. A pair of Mali uromsatyx are shown here.

Brumation

Before uromastyx will breed, they need to experience the seasonal changes that will cue them that it is time to breed. Although uromastyx will sometimes breed without these cues,

It's Better to Wait

Uromastyx should not be bred unless they are at least two years of age. They are capable of breeding much earlier in life, but they should be allowed to mature before going through the stress of brumation, breeding, and laying eggs.

you will get more consistent and productive breeding when your uromastyx do experience the seasonal changes. One method of providing these seasonal cues is to put your lizards through a brumation period. In this sense, brumation is a slight or incomplete hibernation. In complete hibernation, the animal in question sleeps throughout the winter season without waking to feed, defecate, or urinate at all. In brumation, the animal

Only put uros in perfect health through the stress of brumation and mating. This female North African appears to be a good candidate.

may be slightly active. It will not be at its normal activity levels by any means, but it can appear from time to time in order to bask or just move about the enclosure.

Achieving brumation is a task that requires the utmost attention to detail. If brumation is done improperly, it could be a death sentence for your uro. It has been recommended by some that you can simply cut back on the amount of food slowly over a period of time, finally stopping all feeding altogether and then turning off the heat after making sure that the bowels have been evacuated. This is a method that is sometimes used by those who breed snakes, and it can also work with some lizards.

However, this method should never be used when it comes to the uromastyx species. The reason that this method should not be used is that it has led to the death of captive uromastyx because of microbes growing in the hindgut of the uros where undigested food literally rots instead of being digested. Unless you are absolutely sure of the range or area that your particular uromastyx comes from you should refrain from dropping the temperature below the average that would occur in their natural habitat. Even if you are sure of the range, I would be reluctant to drop the temperature severely, as would be the case if you completely shut the heat off. The results could be dire for your uro.

The proper way to brumate uromastyx is to decrease the heat within the enclosure as well as the UVB/UVA exposure and lessen the feeding over a period of time. By doing this, you re-create the gradual changing of the seasons that would be normal in nature. Following the seasons where you live will lead to a successful brumation period. I start to put my uros into brumation in November. The first week in November, I reduce the UV light to eight hours per day. During the second week in November, I reduce the feeding to three times a week. In the third week, I reduce the UV to three to four hours a day and stop feeding the normal fare, only leaving the bean mix.

Within the fourth week reduce the air temperature to the low 70s (roughly 21-23°C) with a night-time drop to about 65° F (18.3°C). During this time, maintain a basking spot of 90 to 95° F (32.2-35°C). This is also the time when you stop feeding altogether. Maintain these conditions for approximately two to three months. When brumating uros, keep the males by themselves. You can keep the females in small groups—three or so—in an appropriately sized enclosure.

Health Matters

The only uromastyx that should be brumated are those that are in exceptional health. This means that throughout the year they have never had any sickness or ailments of any kind. If one of your uros has been sick in the past year, there is a chance that its immune system is still compromised. If you have any doubts about whether or not a uromastyx is healthy enough for brumation, you should hold off brumating that uro until next season. If you put a uromastyx that is less than excellent health into brumation, there is a good chance the lizard will become ill or die.

During brumation, keep a close eye on all the uros but try not to disturb them too much. Although the lizards will spend most of their time in the hide boxes, you should see them emerge once in awhile, typically to bask. If you do not see your uros coming out every three to four days, you should take them out of the hides and check to make sure they haven't dropped drastically in weight or are suffering from some malady. Any uro that appears to be unhealthy during brumation must immediately be removed and placed into an enclosure with normal temperatures. Keep a close watch on the uro; if it does not seem to improve within two days, consult your veterinarian.

Courtship and Mating

After the uros have been brought out of brumation and are feeding regularly for two to three weeks on the regular fare—with extra calcium for the females—it is time to introduce the couples. To do this simply take the male and place him into the female's enclosure. The male will typically taste the substrate a few times, then suddenly realize either by sight or by smell that a female is present. He immediately goes into show-off mode. The most common behavior is rapid push-ups, which many male lizards do to ward off encroaching interlopers or impress females.

The male will also chase the female constantly throughout the cage. If he should catch the female standing still, the male will do a circular dance and spin in place, sometimes for a few minutes at a time with occasional pauses. Whether or not the pausing is to make sure she is watching or to prevent adverse reactions to the spinning is not known

A gravid female white phase ornate uromastyx. Female uromastyx lay eggs about four to six weeks after a successful mating.

Egg Terms

When dealing with egg-laying reptiles and some other egg-laying animals, there are some specific terms used to describe various aspects of their reproduction. Herp hobbyists use these terms all the time, so it is a good idea to become familiar with them.

- A reptile or amphibian that is carrying eggs is said to be *gravid* rather than pregnant.
- A group of eggs laid by one female at one time is called a *clutch*.
- The act of laying the eggs is *oviposition*.
- When the baby reptile has broken through the surface of the egg but is still inside, the egg has *pipped*.

currently. Whatever the case may be it is a very comical display, which can not be done justice by words alone.

In between all of these push-ups and spins, the male will chase the female and attempt to bite her behind the neck, on the nape, and secure her. After he has secured the female he will immediately attempt to copulate with her. During the show put on the by the male, a female will try to hide from the male and run away while he pursues her. This apparently is some type of ritual that they must go through for successful copulation. Usually the male should be left with the female for at least 48 hours in order to assure that insemination has taken place.

If the female is truly not ready for the male's advances, she will flip over onto her back, leaving the male more than likely slightly confused and frustrated. If you should see this behavior, I would immediately remove the male, placing him into either a more receptive female's enclosure or back in his own.

Gestation

If the breeding "took" and the female was inseminated, gestation wll take anywhere from four to six weeks. At this time, the female should be heavily fed with the normal fare as well as extra calcium. Some people recommend feeding insects during this time to increase protein intake; as stated previously, however, uromastyx should not be fed any animal protein.

I don't see the purpose in adding protein at this juncture, because ingesting protein does neither helps nor harms egg production. In fact, a diet heavy in insects may cause kidney stress—organs that are already stressed by the gestation—and this can negatively impact the eggs, not to mention having lasting effects on the health of the female.

Oviposition

While your animals are brumating is a good time to set up the laying or nesting area. That way it will be ready to go when you need it, and you won't have to scramble to set it up at the last minute.

The laying area can be a separate tank you place the female in when she's ready to lay, or you can place a laying box in her normal enclosure. In order to build a laying tank, simply set up a basic enclosure using moistened play sand as the substrate. Add enough moisture so that the sand will hold its shape when you make a tunnel but not so much that it drips when you squeeze a bit of it. This will allow the female to dig a burrow in order to deposit the eggs.

Remove female uromastyx from the nesting box and cage only when you are sure she is finished laying her eggs.

Because keeping a uromastyx in an enclosure with high humidity—as the laying tank would have—poses a risk of respiratory infection, I typically recommend using a laying box instead. To create a laying box, purchase a plastic sweater box with a lid. Cut a hole in the top big enough for the female to fit through, enabling her to crawl inside and deposit the eggs. The box should be partially filled with moistened play sand serving as the laying substrate. Fill the box with enough sand so that the female can move around without having to rub her back on the lid—probably about two-thirds full depending on the box you use.

Before adding the laying box to the enclosure or moving the female to the laying tank, be absolutely sure she is ready to lay her eggs. You can tell this by monitoring her behaviors. You will notice that she is obviously swollen, and she will also begin to look for a place to lay. She will constantly move about the enclosure, digging in various spots.

Sometimes a female will refuse to use both the laying tank and laying box. Instead she will walk about the enclosure and deposit the eggs randomly, only stopping to kick some sand over them. These eggs are not likely to be viable, but you can incubate them anyway and hope for the best. Breeders sometimes suggest trimming the claws of the female's back feet so that she will not rip the eggs when she deposits them and tries to bury them.

Mad Moms!

I have always removed the female before attempting to remove the eggs. The reason for this is that I had a bad experience with a female bearded dragon once. As I was removing her eggs, she attacked me. I suffered some minor scratches and bites. However, ever since that time I have always placed female reptiles into another enclosure before attempting to remove the eggs. Another reason to do so is that the female may be startled by the activity and accidentally trample or jostle the eggs.

If the female does use the laying enclosure or box, she will deposit the eggs and then bury them. Before leaving the eggs she will turn around and ram her head into the damp sand to compact them; this would most likely make it more difficult for predators to uncover them as well as seal in the humidity needed for incubation.

Clutch size depends on the size of the female. Smaller females will lay smaller clutches and larger females will lay larger clutches respectively. The smaller species usually lay approximately a dozen eggs; for the larger species it is more common to see clutches of about 20 eggs.

Incubation

After the eggs are laid and the female has finished covering the nest, you must remove the eggs for artificial incubation. Trying to incubate the eggs in the laying tank or laying box is difficult, and it is unlikely that most of them would survive to hatch. You will have to remove them as soon as possible after laying and place them in an incubator. Removing the eggs from the nest must be done carefully. Always have the incubator set up and ready to go before the eggs hatch. Make sure that it is holding the correct temperature and humidity for at least 48 hours before the eggs hatch.

Recovering the Eggs

If you have not witnessed the female laying the eggs and are not sure of their location, you have to carefully dig throughout the enclosure until the nest is found. When you find it, carefully dig around the entire clutch until it is completely exposed. Then gently take each egg without turning or bumping it in any way and immediately place the group into a container partially filled with incubation medium (usually vermiculite, but other options are discussed later in this chapter) and cover them slightly.

After seven to ten days the eggs will have hardened slightly, at which point you can allow the humidity to drop somewhat. Never add water to the medium during the final incubation stages. This is because the additional water might drown the hatchlings.

It is not difficult to construct your own incubator. The one pictured is for iguana eggs, but the components are the same when incubating uromastyx eggs.

Incubators

Incubation can be done in one of two ways. Either you can build your own incubator or you can use a commercially available incubator. Most of these are made for chicken or other bird eggs, but there are some available specifically for reptiles. You can find the bird ones at farm supply stores, while the Internet is probably the best place to search for a reptile egg incubator.

Building your own incubator is not too difficult. You will need an aquarium or Styrofoam cooler, a submersible aquarium heater, two bricks, a digital thermometer, and a plastic container to hold the incubation medium. To start with, place the bricks in the aquarium or cooler on their sides and then place the thermometer on the opposite side of where you will be placing the heater. Place the heater on the floor of the aquarium and fill the aquarium with water up to just under the top of the bricks. Once the heater is completely submerged you can plug it in and set it to 93°F (33.9°C). Use the digital thermometer to measure the temperature; do not trust the gauge on the heater to be accurate. To cover the incubator and hold in the humidity, you can use a glass aquarium lid or have a piece of Plexiglas cut to fit the top.

Several species of uromastyx have distinct color varieties, called morphs or phases. As an example, here are male white phase (bottom) and navy phase ornate uromastyx (top).

Punch holes in the lid and bottom of the plastic container. Then fill it with your choice

Are You a Good Egg or a Bad Egg?

To ascertain whether an egg is viable, you can candle it. Candling is shining a light through the egg to see whether the embryo is growing. To do this, wrap foil over the end of a bright flashlight and poke a pinhole it. Place the egg in front of the pinhole so the inside of the egg is illuminated. If there is a network of thin lines (the blood vessels), the egg is most likely viable.

of incubation medium; usually about halfway up is fine. You can use vermiculite, perlite, or moistened sand.

Vermiculite is the old standby for most breeders, although getting the ratio of vermiculite to water can be tricky. This medium is not usually sold by pet stores, but you will be able to find it at gardening stores, plant nurseries, and home improvement stores. Sand is another widely used incubation medium. When using sand, you must be aware that the moisture may settle in the bottom, leaving the eggs at the top too dry. Monitor this closely and keep the top layers moist. Perlite is similar to vermiculite and can be used the same way. Like vermiculite, you are more likely to find to perlite in gardening stores than pet stores.

In order for proper incubation, you can either mix seven parts of medium to three parts water by weight or you can simply place an inch or so of the chosen medium into the box and dampen it by spraying. You can also add water to the medium by feel. Add some water to the medium, mix it, and squeeze. If the medium can hold its shape without dripping water, it is moist enough. Place the medium into the plastic box and then make depressions with your thumb where the eggs will be placed. Set this atop the bricks, and you're all set.

When using a commercial incubator, much of the set-up has been done for you. You will have to fill up the reservoir to maintain the proper humidity. Once again, you will have to place the eggs and the incubation medium into some type of plastic container but other than that there is really no work involved. Because there is so little work involved with using a commercial incubator, I recommend using one.

Whether using a homemade or commercial incubator, keep an eye on the moisture level through a good hygrometer placed in the plastic box with the eggs. The humidity should remain between 75 and 85 percent Maintain 93°F (33.9°C) and the humidity level for the 55 to 70 days it takes uromastyx to hatch. Occasionally a clutch can take up to four months, so be patient and don't throw out any eggs unless they have obviously gone bad.

Hatching

At the end of incubation, the babies will slit the egg open using a small projection on the end of their snouts called an egg tooth; this is called pipping. The egg tooth falls off shortly after hatching. The hatchlings may not immediately move out from the egg, and this is fine. This is not the time to panic. You should never attempt to remove the hatchlings from the egg. They may end up staying within the eggs a few days, and they should be left alone.

The reason that hatchlings remain in the egg is to absorb what is left of the yolk, which kept them alive

Hatching ornate uromastyx. Uromastyx eggs usually hatch in 55 to 70 days.

during their time inside the egg. Dragging the yolk around in the desert may lead to serious infection and injury. On occasion a hatchling will come out of the egg before absorbing the yolk completely. Should this occur, take it from the incubator and place it in a sterilized environment on a plain paper towel substrate. The paper towels should be plain white or plain brown, with no dyes or scents. Pile the paper towels up to form some kind of shelter or burrow. Refrain from using any type of décor.

Some breeders use the sterile enclosure for all their hatchlings for up to two weeks in order to facilitate the healing of the site where the yolk was attached. They have cited that the location of the yolk attachment may be susceptible to infection for this period, and they simply choose not to run the risk. Whether you use this type of sterile setup or not is up to you.

As soon as a hatchling comes out of the egg, put it into a proper enclosure at normal

temperatures. This is so it will not disturb any siblings that are still within their eggs. These babies become stressed at the jostling around of their brethren within the incubator.

Hatchling Care

Hatchlings typically can be housed together for the first few weeks without issue. After that time, the yolk site should be completely closed and healed over. If you house the hatchlings together, use a 20- to 30-gallon (75.7-113.6-l) tank and split the hatchlings up into separate groups of three to four individuals.

Set up the hatchling uros as you would the adults, but on smaller scale. This is only after any yolk residue has been absorbed. Most breeders recommend that hatchlings be kept on newspaper, but some use play sand as you would with an

Yemeni uromastyx are sexable soon after hatching. The male is more brightly colored and the female is mostly brown.

You can house hatchling uromastyx in small groups for the first few weeks of their lives. These are hatchling white phase and normal ornate uromastyx.

adult uro. To avoid the risk of impaction, it is best not to keep hatchlings on birdseed. Should you notice that the hatchlings are actually eating rather than incidentally tasting the substrate I would definitely move them onto a newspaper substrate.

Hatchlings in Hand

Handling hatchlings can be a great way to get your new pets to acclimate to human interaction. However, it is important to understand that these hatchlings are very susceptible to injury. During this time their bones are still forming and growing and are considerably softer than those of adults. Therefore, take great care while they are this young so as not to accidentally injure them by rough handling. If they are putting up a struggle to get away from the intruding hand, don't force them to be held. Wait about 15 minutes and then try again. If after a few attempts they simply refuse, it is better to let them rest and try again another day.

As far as feeding goes, some keepers say that hatchlings should be fed appropriate-size crickets once a week. I disagree with this. There is no research to support whether this is a necessity or not and that these lizards are not herbivorous throughout their entire lives. Any hatchlings I have cared for were always offered greens, which were shredded and dusted appropriately. I would also recommend offering at least two separate bowls for feeding greens. The reason for this is to cut down on the possibility of aggressive feeders bullying the smaller ones out of food. Hatchlings should also be offered the same dried bean mix, albeit in ground up form.

Breeders Only!

Some breeders will refuse to sell you certain species (usually ones that are rare in the hobby) unless you plan to breed them. This may seem to be an elitist policy, but it helps ensure that the species will be available for future herpetoculturists to enjoy.

Success!

Should you successfully breed and hatch uromastyx you should be given an award. As of this writing, there probably are fewer than ten breeders who are successfully breeding uros with any regularity. When I think of this, my mentor's words come back to me. I had successfully bred my first corn snakes. I called him to let him know the good news, and in an even tone he said, "Great, now do it again."

After a few more attempts, I discovered why he had said such a thing. It was harder than ever to get those snakes to breed next season. I attribute this to my lack of documentation of the process with which I had success. Therefore, if you plan on breeding uros (or anything for that matter) please do yourself a favor and save the frustration for something else. Document feeding, vitamin and mineral supplement intake, environmental conditions, substrates, etc. It may sound like a lot of nonessential record-keeping, but it is essential if you intend to breed your animals repeatedly. It's wonderful to breed uros once, but only repeated success tells you that you really are doing it right.

Chapter 6

Health Care

Many diseases and ailments can strike a uro without warning. This is especially true when we are speaking of wild-caught uromastyx. Even with captive-born uros, there are health issues that could arise. Most of the diseases and ailments that plague reptiles are directly related to poor husbandry.

If you keep your uro in optimal conditions, you will typically have no issues with diseases and maladies. However, if a disease or injury should occur, under no circumstances should you try to treat it yourself without first consulting a reptile veterinarian.

Parasites

Parasites are the nemesis of reptile keepers. Parasites are more common on wild-caught than on captive-bred uromastyx, but even captive-bred uromastyx can contract parasites through exposure to other infested herps. There are two major types of parasites, internal (called endoparasites) and external (called ectoparasites).

Internal Parasites

Internal parasites normally cannot be seen when you observe your uro, because they live inside the lizard's body, usually in the digestive tract. So how do you know when your uro is infected? Careful observation will give you the first indication that something is awry.

Symptoms of internal parasite infection can differ almost as much as the type of the parasites themselves. Some of the more common symptoms are loss of appetite, vomiting, bloody or runny stools, constipation, weight loss, listlessness, and sunken eyes. Sometimes you may find the parasites or their eggs in your lizard's feces. If your uromastyx shows any of these signs, take the lizard along with a fresh fecal sample to your herp

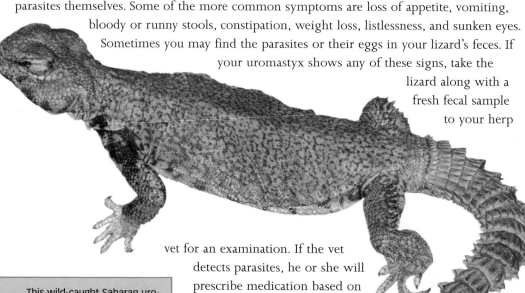

vet for an examination. If the vet detects parasites, he or she will prescribe medication based on the type or types found—wild-caught animals sometimes are carrying several different parasites.

This wild-caught Saharan uromastyx is a bit thin and has closed eyes. Like many wild-caught herps, it needs prompt veterinary care.

External Parasites

External parasites are easier to detect than the internal parasites, but they still pose a serious risk to the health of your lizard if untreated. There are two common external parasites: ticks and mites. Both are bloodsucking arachnids that attach to your lizard's skin. Ticks are almost exclusively found on wild-caught uros, but mites can be found on any lizard because they can crawl from one enclosure to another. Mites are the more serious and difficult to treat of the two types.

Worms and Flukes and Amoebas, Oh My!

There are many different types of internal parasites that infest uromastyx. Some of these include tapeworms, roundworms, flukes, and protozoans (a group that includes amoebas and flagellates). Most wild-caught uromastyx will be carrying one or more of these parasites, so it is important to always take a wild-caught uro to a vet for screening soon after purchase.

Mites These little critters are really small and appear as black-colored little specks crawling over a lizard. Think of them as mosquitoes or lice for reptiles. They have incredibly sharp mouths, which are used to puncture the skin of their reptile host and suck its blood. This on

Finding a Herp Vet

It is not always easy to find vets who are experienced with reptiles and amphibians. Here are some suggestions to help you locate a vet who can help with your pet uromastyx. It is best if you locate one before you actually have an emergency

- Call veterinarians listed as "exotic" or "reptile" vets in the phonebook. Ask them questions to be sure they are familiar with uromastyx.
- Ask at your local pet stores, zoos, animal shelters, and herpetological society— probably your best bet—to see whether there is someone they can recommend.
- Contact the Association of Reptilian and Amphibian Veterinarians. Their website is www.arav.org.

its own wouldn't cause a problem with just one or two mites present. However, they breed like rabbits within the enclosure. So imagine hundreds or even thousands of these bloodsucking creatures devouring the blood of your uro. Given enough time and numbers, mites will severely debilitate your lizard. They may even cause death in small lizards, such as hatchlings.

Mites lay their eggs in the décor and substrate of the enclosure. The mite eggs take around ten days or so to hatch. The newly hatched mites attach themselves to the reptile and continue the cycle. In very little time the number of mites in the enclosure can reach into the thousands. Because they lay eggs in the substrate and furnishings, mites can't be eradicated by treating the reptile alone.

When dealing with mites, you must treat the entire enclosure. A commonly used and successful treatment is a 10 percent solution of bleach and water. To

Mites are especially dangerous to hatchling uros, such as this hatchling Indian uromastyx.

use the bleach solution treatment, you must empty the entire enclosure of its contents. Any non-natural items (e.g., plastic hide boxes) and the enclosure itself should be sprayed with or soaked in the bleach. Let the solution stay on the items for at least 15 minutes, then rinse thoroughly with water. For natural items like wood or stones, place them on a cookie sheet and bake them in the oven at 400°F (204.4°C) for 15 minutes. Put the mite-infested substrate into a garbage bag, then seal the bag and take it outside immediately.

Obviously you will need to also get rid of the mites on the uromastyx itself while you are treating the enclosure and furnishings. There are several methods for doing this. Several miticidal sprays are available at pet stores; they range from useless to highly effective. Talk with local herp keepers to get a recommendation. You may also use any of the household cooking oils as a topical solution. Coat you hands liberally in cooking oil. Hold your uro and allow it to move through your hands. The coating of oil will smother the mites. After the reptile is coated, treat the enclosure and furnishings with a bleach solution as discussed previously. Veterinarians treat mites with a drug called ivermectin.

Mouth Rot

Mouth rot—more correctly called infectious stomatitis—is a common ailment of reptiles. In the early stages it can be seen as excess salivation or as the animal's frequently resting with the mouth open. The inside of the mouth will appear inflamed or red and will often have deposits of cheese-like pus. In the later stages the infection can cause ulcers and swelling to such a degree that the uro can no longer close its mouth or eat. Untreated, it will infect the bone and possibly cause death. Mouth rot usually occurs when a reptile is kept too cool; it also seems to be related to vitamin C deficiencies. Mouth rot is a serious condition. If you suspect you uro has it, seek veterinary attention. Keeping your lizard at the proper temperature and feeding a nutritious diet should prevent this disease.

No-Pest Strips

In the recent past hobbyists would use an insecticidal strip that had been impregnated with the chemical Vapona to kill reptile mites. These products have been implicated in causing illness and even some deaths in treated reptiles. Although the evidence against these strips is circumstantial, I highly recommend against using pest strips in the enclosure or even within the home.

Dermatitis

Many different types of skin afflictions can present themselves. Most dermatological disorders of uros are attributed to a captive environment that is too humid. One specific disease that appears in uromastyx (especially North African uros) is often mistaken for mouth rot. Many cases have shown that the disease is actually hyperkeratotic dermatitis, which is an inflammation of the lip area. This particular disease can also appear on the skin folds of the lizard as well. When it occurs on a uromastyx, it appears as a thickened yellowish patch of moist-looking skin. A uromastyx with dermatitis needs veterinary care.

Respiratory Infections

When uromastyx are not kept at the proper temperatures, they commonly develop respiratory infections. A number of different signs of this problem can occur. A popping sound when breathing and increased or rapid breathing are a couple of the most common signs. Gasping while breathing is also a sure sign that something is wrong with the lizard's respiration. You may also see fluid or mucus in the mouth or nostrils. Such infections are usually treated with antibiotics prescribed by a veterinarian, and typically it takes a long time for the uromastyx to fully recover. It is much easier to simply give the uro the proper environment—high heat and low humidity—in the first place than to treat it for a respiratory infection.

Metabolic Bone Disease

Probably one of the most often-seen diseases in all lizard species in captivity is metabolic bone disease (MBD). Actually more than just one disease, MBD is the term used to describe the signs and symptoms that show up when a reptile has a deficiency of calcium, vitamin D3, or both. Most commonly, the root cause is lack of exposure to UVB lighting, which in turn causes a deficiency of vitamin D3. Without vitamin D3, the lizard will not be able to absorb calcium from its digestive tract and will suffer from a calcium deficiency. Other

Keeping uromastyx too cool or too humid can cause dermatitis and other health issues. A female Mali uromastyx is shown here.

causes include not providing a lizard with enough calcium in its diet, feeding foods that are too high in phosphorus, and kidney disease.

Because the lizard cannot maintain a proper level of calcium in its blood, its body begins to take calcium from its bones. This leads to fragile bones and bone deformities (especially of the jaws and spinal column). The bones often enlarge, giving the appearance that the lizard is fat and healthy. In advanced stages, the lizard suffers from spontaneous fractures,

Cross-Contamination

Cross-contamination occurs when you handle one reptile that has mites or some other illness and then, without washing your hands, you handle another. If one of your herps contracts mites, other parasites, or an infection, you must take steps to prevent cross-contamination. You should move the afflicted animal to a quarantine or hospital enclosure, preferably in another room, away from the rest of your herps. Perform feeding and maintenance of the quarantine cage only after performing it on your other herps. Wash your hands after contact with every enclosure, whether the animals inside are sick or not.

tremors, and seizures. Lizards suffering from MBD may move around very little, because their fractures and deformities are painful and limit mobility. MBD is both debilitating and painful.

If caught early, MBD is somewhat reversible. Some deformities may never be resolved and depending on their severity may mean that euthanizing the uromastyx is the most humane choice for the keeper. Treatment involves addressing the husbandry issues that caused MBD in the first place (poor diet and/or improper lighting usually). The veterinarian may also prescribe injections of calcium and vitamin D3. Any unhealed fractures will also need treatment.

Hypervitaminosis

For whatever reason, many people have some inclination towards excess, believing that if a little is good then more must be better. When applied to uromastyx and vitamin supplementation, this thinking results in hypervitaminosis. Hypervitaminosis is the term for having too much of a vitamin in the body (sometimes it is called vitamin toxicity). In the case of uromastyx and other pet herps, the cause is over-supplementing with vitamins. This is actually easy to do considering we have no way of knowing the proper levels of vitamins, much less what dosages to provide.

Hypervitaminosis refers to too much of any vitamin. In uromastyx, it most often concerns two vitamins, vitamin A and vitamin D3. Excess vitamin A may interfere with the absorption of vitamin D3, which will in turn cause MBD. It is possibly also responsible for organ toxicity of the kidney and the liver. Excessive vitamin D3 can also cause organ toxicity, especially when combined with calcium. Gout is a common disease related to over-supplementation of vitamin D3. Hypervitaminosis D3 can also cause calcium deposits to form in internal organs. Swelling of the throat region is commonly associated with hypervitaminosis of several different vitamins.

It is fairly easy to prevent over-supplementing your uromastyx. Dust the greens so that they have a light coating of powder. You should be able to see the green of the leaves through the powder; don't bury them under a mountain of supplement. Additionally, the best supplements have vitamin A in the form of beta carotene, so the body can convert only as much of this substance into vitamin as it needs. If you suspect your uro has hypervitaminosis, seek veterinary care.

Burns

I have rarely seen any uromastyx that has managed to burn itself. Most often when a uromastyx gets burned it is because an uneducated owner put a hot rock—and usually no other heat source—into the enclosure. The uro lies upon it trying to get warm and becomes burned because of constant contact with the hot stone. Additionally, the wiring of hot rocks is often faulty, causing some spots to become dangerously hot. The result in either case is a horribly scorched uro.

It is also possible for uromastyx to be burned by coming into contact with bulbs or other heat emitters. Because uros (except *U. benti*) are not climbers, they are unlikely to get close enough to the bulbs or emitters to be burned. However, it is possible. Prevent these types of accidents by making sure your uro cannot get to the bulbs and that the temperatures in the enclosure are in the proper range.

A uromastyx that has been burned needs to see a veterinarian right away. These are small animals, so even a burn that appears minor can be quite serious. If the burn is not severe, the vet will clean and dress it and probably prescribe some type of antibiotic or antiseptic

Soft Jaw

Hobbyists often use the term soft jaw (also rubber jaw) to describe lizards suffering from MBD. The reason for this is that the jaw is one of the first bones affected—it bends outwardly as if made of rubber. Additionally, the jaw is often soft to the touch. In severe cases the jaws become so deformed the lizard may have difficulty eating or actually be unable to eat.

North African uromastyx with burn scars. Prevent burns by ensuring your uro cannot come in direct contact with heating apparatus.

salve. More severe burns may require fluids, a hospital stay, or euthanasia.

Wounds

Cuts, nicks, and minor scrapes are inevitable in the wild because of the environment in which uromastyx live. Within the captive environment, however, these problems are easily prevented. Stay away from excessively coarse or rough furnishings. If an object you want to put into the enclosure feels sharp to the skin, it's probably better to discard it and use something else.

If you are using wood, especially sticks, within the enclosure, make sure that it is blunted on the ends so that the uromastyx will not skewer or puncture itself as it wanders the enclosure. A good measure of this is to poke yourself in the hand with the object; if it feels sharp, blunt it down or cut it off. Another way to prevent injury is to place the offending end into the substrate or in a corner where the uro will not encounter it.

If your uro suffers any kind of injury, dab the wound with a cotton swab soaked in hydrogen peroxide and go to a reptile vet as soon as possible.

Over-aggressive breeders can cause injury to one another and therefore should be observed regularly for signs of aggression. Newborns can also be slightly overzealous in their feeding and should be separated at feeding times once they are about three to four weeks old.

Spinal Injuries

Spinal injuries seem to be much more common with uromastyx kept in captivity than in the wild. This probably results from the uro's attempting to climb the glass of the enclosure.

Sometimes during this behavior they bend the spine contrary to the spine's normal range of motion and injure the spinal cord. You can place a perimeter of rocks inside the enclosure, which is a technique I have used before. This for some reason seems to make uros less inclined to attempt to climb the glass.

This behavior seems most common in uromastyx that are kept in a sparsely decorated enclosure. By this I mean one in which no rock piles or hides were offered at all, and the uromastyx being kept were constantly attempting to climb the glass. Once rock piles were built and offered to the uros the behavior stopped literally within hours.

Snout Rubbing

Snout rubbing is a behavior in which a lizard keeps rubbing its face along the walls of its enclosure. While this behavior is not common in uromastyx, it does occasionally occur. Snout rubbing is sometimes attributed to the uro's being in too small an enclosure. While this is a distinct possibility, many believe that uromastyx may perform this behavior because they can not understand that clear glass is a barrier and that their constant rubbing and pushing will do no good in escaping the enclosure.

Preventing snout rubbing is as easy as painting the lower section of the enclosure with an opaque paint. Once the uro cannot see through the glass, the behavior should stop. The paint should be applied to the outside of the terrarium, and the uro should be removed during the process to prevent fumes from entering the enclosure and poisoning your pet.

Become familiar with the appearance and behavior of your uromastyx so you will quickly notice when something is wrong.

We don't know what will happen in terms of the importation of Middle Eastern herps; these areas have suffered more than their share of war and political strife. Therefore it is my sincerest belief that if you do want to purchase a uro as a pet you should please think carefully about the commitment you are undertaking.

Conclusion:
A Tentative Future

Should you want to attempt to breed these incredible agamids, please do so and share the knowledge that you gain through whatever medium possible. In this way we can help to ensure that future herpetoculturists will one day also be capable of discovering the joy of the *Uromastyx* species.

acrodont dentition: having the teeth attached to the top of the jawbone and not sitting in sockets.

brumation: a period of inactivity or torpor in response to unfavorable conditions, such as cool winter temperatures; the animal is not unconscious as in hibernation.

caudal: relating to or near the tail.

cloaca: the common *ventral* opening behind the back legs from which genital, intestinal, and urinary tracts exit the body. The cloaca actually refers to the internal area within the *vent* rather than the opening itself, but is often used interchangeably with the *vent*.

clutch: a group of eggs laid by the same female at the same time.

cutaneous: of or pertaining to the skin, e.g. a cutaneous abscess.

dermatitis: condition in reptiles in which the skin becomes inflamed and is normally caused by keeping the animal in improper conditions.

diurnal: active during the day.

dorsal: relating to the top or back region of an animal.

dystocia: also called *egg-binding*; the situation in which an animal has difficulty laying eggs or giving birth.

ectoparasite: any parasitic organism that is found on the skin of the host organism and attaches itself to feed on the host's blood, e.g. mites and ticks.

ectotherm: an animal that depends on the temperature of its surroundings to regulate its body temperature.

egg-binding: also called *dystocia*; the situation in which an animal has difficulty laying eggs or giving birth.

egg tooth: a small, toothlike projection on the snout of fetal reptiles used to break out of the egg; the egg tooth falls off shortly after hatching.

endoparasite: any parasitic organism that lives inside of the host, e.g. tapeworms.

femoral pores: the row of waxy pores along the underside of the hind legs of most species of uromastyx; pores of males produce a thick waxy secretion which aids in gender determination because they are much larger than those of females.

gravid: the condition in which an animal is carrying developing eggs, whether fertile or infertile.

hatchling: a young reptile that has hatched out of its egg relatively recently; it is usually applied to individuals that less than six months old but it is an inexact term.

helminth: any of the parasitic worms and flukes that are found as *endoparasites* in reptiles and amphibians.

hemipenes: the male uromastyx's mating organ; called such because it is a paired apparatus; each is called a hemipenis.

herbivore: an animal whose diet is comprised of plant matter, often called a vegetarian.

herp: term for reptiles and amphibians collectively, derived from *herpetology*.

herpetoculturist: an individual who studies the captive care and husbandry of reptiles and amphibians.

herpetologist: an individual who studies the branch of zoology comprising reptiles and amphibians.

herpetology: the branch of zoology comprised of reptiles and amphibians.

hindgut: the rear portion of the alimentary canal in uromastyx; this is where digestion of cellulose (plant matter) takes place.

host: the organism in which or on which a parasite lives and derives nourishment.

impaction: condition in which some material—often the cage substrate—is blocking up the digestive tract.

Jacobson's organ: sensory apparatus at the roof of a lizard's mouth that detects both scent and taste.

juvenile: a young herp that has not reached sexual maturity.

metabolic bone disease (MBD): a term to describe a severe lack of calcium leading to brittle and deformed bones and neurological disorders.

ocellus: circular, eye-like spots. The plural is *ocelli* and the adjective form is *ocellated*.

omnivore: an animal that consumes of both plant and animal matter.

oviposition: the process of laying eggs.

oxalic acid: a compound naturally occurring in many plants, which if eaten in excess can lead to metabolic bone disease (MBD) and gout.

parietal eye: also called the "third eye", this is a light sensitive spot on the top of the uromastx's head between its eyes. It is thought to play an important role in thermoregulation and reproductive behavior.

pleurodont dentition: having the teeth attached to the inside of the jawbone and not sitting in sockets.

salmonella: a class of bacteria that occur naturally in the gut of most reptiles including uromastyx. If transmitted in high concentrations to humans can lead to serious health problems particularly in immuno-compromised individuals.

saurian: a lizard; derived from Sauria, the suborder in which lizards are placed.

SVL (snout-to-vent length): the length between the tip of the snout and the *vent* immediately behind the back legs. Commonly used to measure reptiles because they so frequently lose some part of their tail, and SVL is proportional to total length.

thermoregulation: altering body temperature to the preferred temperature; uromastyx are *ectotherms* and they thermoregulate by using warm or cool areas in their environment.

third eye: a basic lens on top of the head between the eyes, also called the *parietal eye*. Used to detect changes in light level and intensity. It mainly plays a role during thermoregulation and in detecting seasonal changes.

tympanum: the exposed ear drum on each side of the head behind the eyes; also called the *tympanic membrane*.

vent: the actual opening where waste products from the *cloaca* are expelled from the body, and from which the male extrudes his *hemipenes* during mating. It can be seen as a slit on the underside of the tail immediately behind the back legs.

ventral: the underside or belly. This, naturally enough, is where you'll find the *vent*.

zoonosis: a disease that can pass from animals to humans, e.g. salmonella.

Ask the Vet—Vitamins. http://www.beardeddragon.org/articles/vitamins/.

BBC. The Care and Breeding of Spiny-Tailed Lizards. http://www.bbc.co.uk/dna/h2g2/a947162

Cunningham P. L. Daily Activity Pattern and Diet of a Population of the Spiny-Tailed Lizard, *Uromastyx aegyptius microlepis*, during summer in the United Arab Emirates. *Zoology in the Middle East* 21 (2000): 37-46

Cunningham, P. L. Notes on the Diet, Survival Rate, and Burrow Specifics of *Uromastyx aegyptius microlepis* from the United Arab Emirates. *Asiatic Herpetological Research*. 9 (2001): 30-33

Gerhmann, William H. Reptile Lighting: a Current Perspective. *The Vivarium*. 8(2) (1997): 44-45, 62.

Gray, Randall L. Captive Husbandry of Ornate Spiny-Tailed Lizards.
http://www.kingsnake.com/uromastyx/caresheets/ornate.htm

Gray, Randall L. Captive Reproduction of "Rainbow benti" Spiny-Tailed Lizards (*Uromastyx benti*).
http://www.kingsnake.com/uromastyx/urocaresheet.html

Jones, J. R., Ferguson, G. W., Gehrinann, W. H., Holick, M. F., Chen, T. C., and Z. Lu. Vitamin D nutritional status influences voluntary behavioral photoregulation in a lizard. 1996. In, *Biologic Effects of Light*. 1995. M. F. Holick and E. G. Jung (eds.) Walter de Gruyter, N. Y.

Kaplan, Melissa. Musings on D3 and UV… 2002. http://www.anapsid.org/uvd3.html

Minton, Sherman A. A Contribution to the Herpetology of West Pakistan. Bulletin of the AMNH. 134 (1966): article 2

Moehn Loren D. The Effect of Light on Agnostic Behavior of Iguanid and Agamid Lizards. *Journal of Herpetology*. 8(2) (1974):175-183

Reptile Database. Uromastyx ornata.
http://www.tigr.org/reptiles/species.php?genus=Uromastyx&species=ornata

Sahara Nature. Uromastyx alfredschmidti. http://www.sahara-nature.com/animaux.php?species=uromastyx_alfredschmidti

Sorin, Eric and Sorin, Suzy. Karnivor's Care Sheet for the Genus *Uromastyx*.
http://www.kingsnake.com/uromastyx/urocaresheet.html

UVB Fluorescent Tubes. http://www.uvguide.co.uk/fluorescenttuberesults.htm

Walls, Jerry G. *The Guide to Owning Uromastyx and Butterfly Agamids*. Neptune City, NJ: T.F.H. Publications, Inc.

Wilms, T. and Boehme, W. Revision der Uromastyx acantinura—Artengruppe, mit Beschreibung einer neuen Art aus der Zentralsahara (Reptilia: Sauria: Agamidae). *Zool. Abh. Staatl. Mus. Tierk. Dresden*. 51 (2000): 73-104

Clubs & Societies

Amphibian, Reptile & Insect Association
Liz Price
23 Windmill Rd
Irthlingsborough
Wellingborough NN9 5RJ
England

American Society of Ichthyologists and Herpetologists
Maureen Donnelly, Secretary
Grice Marine Laboratory
Florida International University
Biological Sciences
11200 SW 8th St.
Miami, FL 33199
Telephone: (305) 348-1235
E-mail: asih@fiu.edu
www.asih.org

Society for the Study of Amphibians and Reptiles (SSAR)
Marion Preest, Secretary
The Claremont Colleges
925 N. Mills Ave.
Claremont, CA 91711
Telephone: 909-607-8014
E-mail: mpreest@jsd.claremont.edu
www.ssarherps.org

Veterinary Resources

Association of Reptile and Amphibian Veterinarians (ARAV)
P.O. Box 605
Chester Heights, PA 19017
Phone: 610-358-9530
Fax: 610-892-4813
E-mail: ARAVETS@aol.com
www.arav.org

Rescue And Adoption Services

Las Cruces Reptile Rescue
www.awesomereptiles.com/lcrr/rescueorgs.html

New England Amphibian and Reptile Rescue
www.ReptileRescue.net

Petfinder.com
www.petfinder.org

Reptile Rescue, Canada
http://www.reptilerescue.on.ca

RSPCA (UK)
Wilberforce Way
Southwater
Horsham, West Sussex RH13 9RS
Telephone: 0870 3335 999
www.rspca.org.uk

WEBSITES

Basic Care for Uromastyx
http://www.exoticpetvet.com/breeds/iguanageckos1.htm

Herp Station
http://www.petstation.com/herps.html

Kingsnake.com
http://www.kingsnake.com/beardeddragons

The Lizard Lounge
www.the-lizard-lounge.com

Melissa Kaplan's Herp Care Collection
http://www.anapsid.org/

Reptile Forums
http://reptileforums.com/forums/

Reptile Rooms, The
http://www.reptilerooms.org

Uromastyx Home Page, The
http://www.kingsnake.com/uromastyx/

MAGAZINES

Reptiles Magazine
P.O. Box 6050
Mission Viejo, CA 92690
www.animalnetwork.com/reptiles

Reptile Care
Mulberry Publications, Ltd.
Suite 209 Wellington House
Butt Road, Colchester
Essex, CO3 3DA
United Kingdom

***Reptilia* Magazine**
Salvador Mundi 2
Spain-08017 Barcelona
Subscripciones-subscriptions@reptilia.org

Note: **Boldfaced** numbers indicate illustrations; an italic t indicates tables.

About the Author:

John F. Taylor has been actively involved in herpetoculture for more than a decade. He has experience keeping and breeding over 100 species of reptiles, including uromastyx and other agamid lizards; he has written many articles on reptile husbandry. John has acted as a hired consultant for commercial uromastyx breeding projects. He lives in the San Diego area with his fiancé and son.

Photo Credits:

R. D. Bartlett: 18, 26, 30, 44, 66, 68, 78, 85 (center), 106,
Eric Isselee (courtesy of Shutterstock): 3, 41, 119
Isabelle Francais: 9, 37, 40, 49, 50, 51, 52, 55, 62, 70, 80, 82, 84 (top), 92, and back cover
Paul Freed: 20, 25, 53, 85 (top), 87, 104, 109, 122
U. E. Friese: 112
Patrick LeFebvre (animals courtesy of Audrey Vanderlinden): 1, 4, 16, 19, 23, 33, 38, 42, 58, 61, 67, 72, 84 (bottom),
85 (bottom), 88, 90, 95, 97, 98, 100, 102, 113, 114
W. P. Mara: 28, 36, 47
Aaron Norman: 21,
Alexander Shalamov (courtesy of Shutterstock): 10
Karl H. Switak: 6, 12, 13, 14, 57, and cover
Maleta M. Walls: 35, 64, 75, 77